# WALC™ 9: Verbal and Vi‹

## Workbook of Activities for Language and Cognition

### by Kathryn J. Tomlin

### Skills

- verbal and visual reasoning
- thought organization
- convergent reasoning
- logic
- insight
- integration
- inferencing
- visual perception

### Ages

- 16 and up

### Grades

- high school and up

### Evidence-Based Practice

According to the *Clinical Guidelines of The Royal College of Speech & Language Therapists* (www.rcslt.org/resources, 2005) and the National Stroke Association (2006), the following therapy principles are supported:

- Communication, both verbal and nonverbal, is a fundamental human need. Meeting this need by facilitating and enhancing communication in any form can be vital to a patient's well-being.
- Therapy should include tasks that focus on semantic processing, including semantic cueing of spoken output, semantic judgments, categorization, and word-to-picture matching.
- Therapy may target the comprehension and production of complex, as well as simple, sentence forms.
- Therapy should be conducted within natural communication environments.
- Rehabilitation is an important part of recovering from a stroke, and the goal is to regain as much independence as possible.

This book incorporates the above principles and is also based on expert professional practice.

**LinguiSystems®**

LinguiSystems, Inc.
3100 4th Avenue
East Moline, IL 61244

FAX: 800-577-4555
Phone: 800-776-4332
E-mail: service@linguisystems.com
Web: linguisystems.com

Copyright © 2007 LinguiSystems, Inc.

All of our products are copyrighted to protect the fine work of our authors. You may only copy the client materials needed for your own use. Any other reproduction or distribution of the pages in this book is prohibited, including copying the entire book to use as another source or "master" copy.

The enclosed CD is for your personal use and convenience. It is unlawful to copy this CD or store its contents on a multi-user network.

Printed in the U.S.A.

ISBN 978-0-7606-0750-3

# About the Author

Kathy and her therapy dog, Zanmi

**Kathryn J. Tomlin**, M.S., CCC-SLP, has been a speech-language pathologist in hospitals, rehabilitation centers, and long-term care facilities for over 25 years. Her materials, developed while working with clients, have evolved over the years. She has authored many materials with LinguiSystems over the last 20 years. Some of her works include:

*The Source for Apraxia Therapy*
*WALC (Workbook of Activities for Language and Cognition) Series—*
- *WALC 1: Aphasia Rehab (English and Spanish versions)*
- *WALC 2: Cognitive Rehab (English and Spanish versions)*
- *WALC 8: Word Finding*
- *WALC 10: Memory*
- *WALC 11: Language for Home Activities*

Zanmi, Kathy's Samoyed, goes to work with her to encourage clients. Her clients enjoy feeding and spending time with Zanmi, and Zanmi enjoys their company. Everybody wins!

# Dedication

This book is dedicated to the "Peanut Gallery" at Liberty Nursing & Rehabilitation Center: Kathy Kattner, Hollie Gower, Alison Parker, Lois Steward, Dawn Villanova, Lisa Yerger, Jennifer Klembara, Liz Buresh, Kim Sturm, and Gail Combs. I am most grateful for your input on these exercises and during my therapy sessions. Believe it or not, I am listening to your input more than I will ever let you know. You're the best!

*Edited by Lauri Whiskeyman*
*Cover Design by Jason Platt*
*Illustrations by Margaret Warner*
*Page Layout by Lisa Parker*

# Table of Contents

▶ **Introduction** ........................................................... 7

▶ **Verbal Reasoning** ...................................................... 10

  **Emotions and Personal Situations** ..................................... 10

    Emotions—Describing Situations ..................................... 11
    Situations—Labeling Emotions ....................................... 12
    Consequences ....................................................... 13
    Causes ............................................................. 14
    Problem Solving—Missing Equipment .................................. 15
    Opinions ........................................................... 17
    Self-Concept ....................................................... 18
    Self-Analysis ...................................................... 19
    Family Interaction ................................................. 20
    Wishes ............................................................. 21
    Employment Analysis ................................................ 22
    Friendship ......................................................... 23
    The Perfect Day .................................................... 24
    Ten Enjoyable Activities ........................................... 25
    Activity Goals ..................................................... 26
    Conversation Skills ................................................ 27

  **Idioms and Proverbs** .................................................. 36

    Expression Completion and Explanation .............................. 37
    Missing Letters .................................................... 39
    Mixed-Up Expressions ............................................... 40
    Expression Interpretation—Literal and Abstract ..................... 41
    Matching Proverbs to Situations .................................... 44

  **Categorization** ....................................................... 45

    Naming Objects by Attributes ....................................... 46
    Description—One Object ............................................. 49
    Description and Comparison—Two Objects ............................. 51
    Which Does Not Belong? ............................................. 53
    General Category Labeling .......................................... 55
    Subcategory Labeling ............................................... 56
    Specific Member Labeling ........................................... 57
    Categorization Grid ................................................ 58
    Categorization in Sentences ........................................ 60

**Table of Contents**, continued

## Convergent Reasoning .... 61

Fact/Opinion .... 62
Negative True/False Statements .... 64
Sequencing .... 66
Increasing Word Length .... 69
Diagrams with Choices .... 70
Diagrams Without Choices .... 73
Anagrams .... 75
Anagrams in Sentences .... 77
Symbol Substitution .... 79
Change One Letter .... 81
Change One Letter—Create .... 83
Numbers and General Information .... 84
Double Meaning Deduction .... 85
Deduction Puzzles .... 87
Roman Numeral Conversion .... 93
Deduction by Exclusion .... 94
Word Search—Opposites .... 96
Logic Questions .... 97
Word Wheel .... 101
Build the Answer .... 102
Combined Associated Words .... 103
Separating .... 105
Numerical Sequences .... 107
Acrostics .... 109
Describe Without Naming .... 111
Advertisements .... 112

## Analogies .... 113

Completing Analogies .... 114
Analogies—Complete the Second Half .... 115
Analogies—Complete the First Section .... 118

## Paragraph Comprehension .... 120

Story Inferences .... 121

**Table of Contents**, continued

## ▶ Visual Reasoning .................................................... 124

### Visual Analogies .................................................... 124
Picture Analogies .................................................... 125
Figural Analogies—One Factor ........................................ 129
Figural Analogies—Two Factors ....................................... 132
Figural Analogies—Three Factors ..................................... 135
Drawing Analogy Pairs—One Factor ................................... 138
Drawing Analogy Pairs—Two Factors .................................. 140

### Visual Figure-Ground ............................................... 142
Locating Items ...................................................... 143
Embedded Shapes ..................................................... 146

### Visual Sequencing .................................................. 150
Figural Sequences—One Factor ........................................ 151
Figural Sequences—Two Factors ....................................... 153
Figural Sequences—Three Factors ..................................... 155
Figural Sequences—Varying Number of Factors ......................... 156
Connect the Dots—Alphabetical ....................................... 158
Connect the Dots—Numerical .......................................... 159
Connect the Dots—Alternating ........................................ 160
Connect the Dots—Integration ........................................ 161

### Visual Closure and Reasoning ....................................... 162
Closure ............................................................. 163
Mirror Images ....................................................... 165
Figural Grid ........................................................ 167
Differences Between Pictures ........................................ 169
Picture Inferences .................................................. 173
Picture Incongruities ............................................... 177

### Drawing ............................................................ 180
Directions—Grid ..................................................... 181
Draw Figure to Scale ................................................ 182
Floor Plan Sketch ................................................... 183

## ▶ Resources ........................................................... 185

## ▶ Answer Key ......................................................... 187

# Introduction

Being able to reason with verbal and visual information is an integral part of how we communicate, problem solve, make decisions, and achieve success in relationships with others. The tasks in *WALC 9: Verbal and Visual Reasoning* address multiple levels of reasoning in a wide variety of exercises. This is to improve your client's ability to reason flexibly and to expand his ability to identify, analyze, and modify information. Having a large repertoire of verbal and visual reasoning abilities will help your client determine the effectiveness of his own responses plus analyze what is being said to him or presented to him in written or graphic form.

*WALC 9* was written to provide stimulus materials for verbal and visual reasoning when working with clients who are neurologically impaired. The tasks in this book, developed while working with a wide variety of clients, have evolved and have been perfected over the years. The tasks will stimulate your client's ability to reason while tapping into many facets of cognitive-linguistic communication. He will use pre-existing skills (i.e., previously learned visual and verbal content and processes already established in a client's cognitive system) to help him link or associate information as a basis for solving the challenging, integrative tasks.

Verbal and visual reasoning tasks are the main focus of this book, however many processes are addressed in each task, including the following.

- **Thought Organization**
  Most of the tasks in this book involve organization of thought (e.g., strategies that require your client to determine a relationship or process and carry that pattern over to successfully complete similar tasks). Being able to think in a logical, organized manner will improve your client's ability to reason.

- **Convergent Reasoning**
  Being able to think convergently will help your client stay on topic as he zeroes in on a response using information given (e.g., answering logic questions).

- **Logic**
  When a person has difficulty with reasoning, his line of logical thinking can become tangential and/or completely unrelated. The tasks in this book are designed to present information in a logical manner in such a way as to stimulate logical thought for solving the tasks correctly. The patterns will become established in your client's cognitive abilities and the process will transfer to problem solving for various situations and activities in daily life.

- **Insight**
  Being able to determine if your actions or responses are appropriate is a skill that is necessary for successful reasoning. The tasks in this book are designed to give your client insight into why a response may be wrong and to use that insight to try again and/or to understand the correct answer. Your client's insight will improve when he successfully completes a task or when he analyzes an answer's correctness by comparing it to the responses in the answer key.

**Introduction**, *continued*

- **Integration**
  Every person has a preexisting knowledge base and reasoning style. As we go through each day, it is important to perceive new information and to integrate salient information into our patterns of thinking. Frequently someone who has a neurological impairment will be very reluctant to integrate new information. The tasks in this book are designed to stimulate the need for integration of new information in order to be successful in answering questions or solving tasks.

- **Inferencing**
  Many of the tasks in this book involve the skill of being able to make an inference. Effective reasoning can only occur if your client is able to read between the lines when listening to verbal information or to make the correct judgment when interpreting visual information.

- **Visual Perception**
  For your client's reasoning abilities to be effective, it is important that he visually perceives information in the correct manner. If something is perceived incorrectly, then problem solving, deduction, and reasoning will be negatively affected. The tasks in this book provide various levels of visual stimuli (e.g., shapes, figures, pictures) to improve your client's ability to see visual stimuli correctly and to make the correct interpretation of the material.

Verbal and visual reasoning skills can be compromised if your client has poor conversation skills. It is important that a person is able to receive all necessary input and to share what he feels he is having difficulty with. The tasks in the conversation skills section of the book insure that your client is receiving information accurately, utilizing nonverbal information to aid reasoning, balancing speaker/listener skills, answering questions effectively, and verbally expressing himself in an effective manner.

Many of the tasks in this book involve working with words, so as your client progresses through the book, his vocabulary will improve. A broad vocabulary can assist with reasoning skills.

**Suggestions for Use**

1. Initially, the majority of these exercises will be difficult. Keep in mind that you're aiding the client in developing different thinking processes as opposed to striving for 100% accuracy. It's strongly suggested that you familiarize yourself with each exercise so you can help the client throughout the training period before expecting the client to complete the exercise independently. Be prepared to give cues or even the answers to stimulate the client's learning abilities.

2. Reassure your client that it's not as important for him to answer each item as it is for him to be able to utilize strategies for solving the items within a task.

**Introduction**, *continued*

3. Determine the appropriateness of responses based on the client's current level of cognitive functioning. Consider shaping approximations over successive trials or sessions. Emphasize enjoyment in the challenge rather than accuracy.

4. These exercises can be used in individual or group situations. In group situations, clients can work together to solve the problems or take turns providing answers, thus giving each other valuable feedback. Encourage the client to work with his family on the exercises.

5. The exercises may be used for stimulus of intentional memory strategies. When it's necessary for you to provide an answer, explain to the client that you'll be asking him to later recall the answer and to intentionally code the answer. If necessary, aid the client's coding by providing him with auditory or visual strategies he may use, depending on his strongest method for coding input.

6. These exercises can also be used to stimulate incidental memory strategies. At the end of a task, ask the client to recall methods he used, the format of the task, or salient content that was provided. If you do this consistently, the client will begin to anticipate what you may ask for, thus indirectly providing practice with the automatic use of memory strategies.

7. As the client learns the strategies or processes necessary for solving the tasks, the level of difficulty can be increased by asking the client to create similar items for you to solve. This gives him the chance to create and be flexible. This experience can be challenging and enjoyable for both you and your client. The client will learn much from this creative process.

8. The exercises are not for testing purposes. Try to make them as enjoyable as possible. Talking about specific task items will help your client improve his ability to identify, create, and modify strategies.

9. The answers in the Answer Key are provided as a reference. There are times when items have multiple answers even if only one is listed. Accept other, appropriate answers as correct.

*WALC 9* provides a wide variety of thinking and reasoning stimulus materials. Share *WALC 9* with the client's family to establish the importance of improving communication outside of the therapy setting. As you use these exercises, it's my hope that you'll discover the unending uses for and versatility of these tasks.

May you enjoy the adventure of working with language and cognitive communication skills as much as I do.

Kathy

# Verbal Reasoning

Verbal reasoning is a key element when communicating with others, solving problems, and making decisions. For effective verbal reasoning, a client needs to think logically, offer insight into whether something is right or wrong, integrate new information, and make inferences. The tasks in this section address multiple levels of verbal reasoning to improve your client's ability to think flexibly and to analyze information. Even though many of the tasks may be challenging for your client, they provide ample opportunity for discussion, which will further help your client improve his reasoning abilities. The skills your client uses when completing the activities in this section will improve his reasoning abilities in his daily life.

# Emotions and Personal Situations

The tasks on pages 11-35 include activities on emotions, personal situations, and conversation skills. As your client works with these tasks, he will expand and improve his verbal reasoning skills.

When a client has had a change in his brain function, the ability to perceive, interpret, and respond to emotions is frequently impaired. His world tends to get limited to three emotions (happy, sad and angry) and he loses the ability to determine how changes in situations affect people's actions and responses. In personal situations, he may have difficulty seeing beyond the obvious. The tasks in this section will aid your client in reestablishing his repertoire of emotions and problem-solving skills and help him improve his ability to look beyond himself in various situations. At times, the tasks will apply directly to him. Other components of the tasks will require him to focus on other people or situations. The tasks are formatted to improve organization and to provide a structure for reorganizing personal information.

Impairment in verbal reasoning can have a negative impact on a client's ability to converse effectively. The conversation tasks are designed to help bring your client's skills back into balance. This way, he can receive all necessary information for effective reasoning and ask for clarifying information or discuss the processes he is relearning or needs help relearning. Effective verbal reasoning requires balanced speaker-listener skills, being able to converse in an organized manner, being able to interpret verbal and nonverbal information, being able to attend over time, and asking questions in order to insure all salient information has been received.

Your client's verbal reasoning skills will be negatively affected if he cannot identify emotional content, look beyond himself or the concrete nature of objects, or utilize effective conversation skills. These tasks will help in the identification of stimuli so that he can verbally reason effectively to determine a course of action or participate effectively in communication.

## Emotions—Describing Situations

Describe situations in which a person would feel these ways.

1. happy
2. enthusiastic
3. enraged
4. amazed
5. nervous
6. embarrassed
7. panicked
8. sad
9. relieved
10. scared
11. lonely
12. brave
13. anxious
14. bored
15. depressed
16. disgusted
17. contented
18. ashamed
19. confused
20. worried
21. expectant
22. irritated
23. kind
24. confident
25. angry
26. satisfied
27. disappointed
28. sympathetic
29. neglected
30. impressed
31. helpless
32. silly
33. cheated
34. weary
35. joyful
36. lucky
37. empathetic
38. excited
39. hopeful
40. refreshed

# Situations—Labeling Emotions

Tell how the person or people would feel in each situation. Do not use the feelings *happy*, *sad*, or *angry*.

1. a child at a circus
2. a wife whose husband just died
3. a runner before a race
4. someone graduating from high school or college
5. an adolescent whose parents said he could not go out with his friends on a weekend night
6. a spectator whose football team just scored a touchdown
7. an officer leading his men into battle
8. a person who has no friends and nowhere to go
9. a soon-to-be father whose wife is in labor
10. a babysitter who hears noises outside
11. parents who just received word that their child was in a car accident
12. a person trapped in an elevator
13. someone who told a lie and was found out
14. a baby who is dry, was just fed, and is being held by his mother
15. a person at a job interview
16. the winner of a million dollar lottery
17. a person who has difficulty remembering names and events
18. a person listening to a two-hour lecture on something he is not interested in
19. a mother whose children are grown up and have moved away
20. a family relocating to another state

## Consequences

Tell what can happen in each situation.

1. being unsanitary
2. forgetting to pay your bills
3. a hit-and-run accident
4. having an immature babysitter
5. not keeping up with car maintenance
6. not locking the car
7. following peer pressure
8. overusing credit cards
9. too many people in one area
10. not trying on clothes before you buy them
11. speeding
12. a child in competitive sports
13. not being immunized
14. children playing with matches
15. taking pictures of a group
16. talking on the phone while dinner is cooking
17. drinking and driving
18. not locking the doors of your residence
19. not getting yearly checkups
20. lying

# Causes

Tell what could cause each event.

1. a river overflowing
2. a friend refusing to talk to you
3. being stranded in your house
4. divorce
5. receiving a phone call at three o'clock in the morning
6. a car needing mechanical work
7. a chair needing reupholstering
8. getting a phone call from a friend
9. a bounced check
10. a flat tire
11. becoming a millionaire
12. going to the dentist
13. a dog barking
14. wearing a hat
15. the circuit breaker tripping
16. a house catching on fire
17. a child running away from home
18. a country going to war
19. being stopped by a police officer
20. needing a prescription filled

# Problem Solving—Missing Equipment

Solve these problems. Assume that you have access to other objects.

1. You need to change a ceiling light, but you do not have a ladder.
2. You locked your keys in the car and do not have a spare set.
3. You have to remove a screw, but you do not have a screwdriver.
4. There is something on fire in the oven, and you do not have a fire extinguisher.
5. You have to tie up tomato plants, but you do not have any stakes.
6. You have to prop a door open, but you do not have a wedge.
7. You have to cross a creek, but there is no bridge.
8. The zipper breaks on your pants, and you do not have a pin.
9. You need to cut paper in half, but you do not have any scissors.
10. You go to get a drink, but there are no cups.
11. Your filing cabinet is locked, and you have lost the key.
12. You need to open a can, but you do not have a can opener.
13. You need to copy a report, but the copy machine is broken.
14. You are in a hotel and need to hang up your clothes, but there are no hangers.
15. Your child cannot reach the table, and you do not have a high chair.
16. You need to join five pieces of paper together, but you do not have a stapler.
17. You want to cover a table, but you do not have a tablecloth.
18. You are camping and have to keep your food cold, but you do not have ice or a cooler.
19. You need to remove a heavy-duty staple from a shipping box, but you do not have a staple remover.
20. You need a light in the woods, but you do not have a flashlight.

# Problem Solving—Missing Equipment

Solve these problems. Assume that you have access to other objects.

1. You need to carry water, but you do not have a bucket.
2. You need to stir a can of paint, but you do not have a stirrer.
3. You need to get something out from under a piece of furniture that you cannot lift, and you cannot reach it with your hand.
4. You need to remove a cork from a bottle, but you do not have a corkscrew.
5. You need to carry several objects, but you do not have a bag.
6. You need to walk your dog, but you do not have a leash.
7. You need to start a fire, but you do not have a match.
8. You need to remove paint from a window pane, but you do not have paint remover.
9. You need to open a padlock, but you do not have the key.
10. You need to trim bushes, but you do not have shears.
11. You want to play football, but you do not have a football.
12. You want to prevent a door from opening, but you do not have a lock.
13. You want to block the sun from coming in a window, but you do not have curtains.
14. You want to burn a candle, but you do not have a candle holder.
15. You want to go fishing, but you do not have a pole.
16. You want to cover a can, but you do not have a lid.
17. You need to draw a straight line, but you do not have a ruler.
18. You want to draw a circle, but you do not have a compass.
19. You want to keep dry in the rain, but you do not have an umbrella.
20. You want to eliminate a pen mark, but you do not have an eraser.

# Opinions

Give your opinion about the following topics.  All opinions are accepted.

1. smoking
2. divorce
3. men doing housework
4. integrated schools
5. factory work
6. charge cards
7. holidays
8. television
9. hobbies
10. newspapers
11. gambling
12. restaurants
13. friendship
14. unemployment compensation
15. public schools
16. politics
17. life insurance
18. speed limits
19. car racing
20. religion
21. welfare
22. hospitalization
23. competitive sports
24. the stock market
25. common-law marriage
26. the draft
27. guns
28. designated smoking areas
29. airline travel
30. jogging
31. abortion
32. illegal drugs
33. a woman president
34. wearing seatbelts
35. capital punishment
36. working the night shift
37. country living
38. child abuse
39. raising children
40. rock music

*Verbal Reasoning—Emotions and Personal Situations*
*WALC 9: Verbal and Visual Reasoning*

# Self-Concept

Follow the directions or answer the questions.

1. List ten words that describe yourself.

2. List ten words that describe each of your family members.

3. How do you spend your free time?

4. What are your goals five years from now? in 10 years? in 20 years?

5. List the qualities of people you admire.

6. What are your favorite sports and hobbies?

7. What is your favorite TV show? Favorite movie?

8. What values are very important to you?

9. How would your parents have described you as a child?

10. What is your favorite possession?

# Self-Analysis

Follow these directions regarding information about yourself.

1. List three characteristics about yourself that you admire.

   A.

   B.

   C.

2. List three characteristics about yourself that you do not admire.

   A.

   B.

   C.

3. Explain how you could change the qualities that you do not admire.

   A.

   B.

   C.

# Family Interaction

Follow these directions regarding information about your family.

1. Describe your family's greatest achievement.

2. Describe one specific thing about each member in your family.

3. Name three things your family enjoys doing together.

4. Name one thing your family could do to improve life at home.

5. Name three ways your family makes you feel happy.

6. Name three things you do for your family.

7. Name three things your family does for you.

# Wishes

Write four wishes you would like to have come true for yourself. Then write four wishes for four other people you know.

**Yourself**

1.
2.
3.
4.

**Person 1:** _____

1.
2.
3.
4.

**Person 2:** _____

1.
2
3.
4.

**Person 3:** _____

1.
2.
3.
4.

**Person 4:** _____

1.
2.
3.
4.

# Employment Analysis

List the skills needed for the type of job you want. Determine what areas you must work on to fulfill the responsibilities for the job.

1. **Health and Physical Skills Needed:** (coordination, fine and gross motor skills, stamina, strength, speed, visual skills, health status, etc.)

2. **Intellectual Skills Needed:** (ability to learn new information, reading and writing skills, problem solving skills, memory, attention span, ability to follow instructions, independence, etc.)

3. **Interpersonal Skills Needed:** (ability to follow and lead, cooperation, self-control, politeness, personal appearance, level of independence, etc.)

4. **Self-Management Skills Needed:** (seeking assistance, detecting problems, prioritizing, managing time, persistence, maintaining motivation, etc.)

# Friendship

Answer the following questions.

1. Tell how you and your friends are alike.

2. Tell how you and your friends are different.

3. What qualities are important for a friend to possess?

4. How would you tell a friend that there is something about his/her personality you do not like?

5. If your friends were doing something that you did not wish to be involved in, how would you tell them?

6. Apply this expression to friendship: "Birds of a feather flock together."

7. Apply this expression to friendship: "A friend in need is a friend indeed."

8. Apply this expression to friendship: "Opposites attract."

9. Explain why a friendship between you and someone else ended.

10. Discuss the positive and negative qualities of your best friend.

# The Perfect Day

Use your imagination to plan the perfect day.

1. Where will it take place?

2. When will it happen?

3. What will the weather be?

4. Who else will be involved?

5. What will you do?

6. What equipment will you need?

7. What food will you need?

8. How will you get there?

9. What clothing will you wear?

10. How will you end the day?

# Ten Enjoyable Activities

List 10 things you like to do. Then state how much each activity costs and when you last did it.

| Activity | Cost | When I last did it |
|---|---|---|
| 1. | | |
| 2. | | |
| 3. | | |
| 4. | | |
| 5. | | |
| 6. | | |
| 7. | | |
| 8. | | |
| 9. | | |
| 10. | | |

# Activity Goals

Plan four activities using this organization guide.

| What I want to do | What I will need | Other people involved | Things that have to be done | Completion date |
|---|---|---|---|---|
| 1. | | | | |
| 2. | | | | |
| 3. | | | | |
| 4. | | | | |

# Conversation Skills—Speaker-Listener

Being a good listener is as important as being a good speaker. When you talk with others, you'll usually listen more than you speak. Here are a few things to remember to do and not to do.

**Do:**
- ✓ Pay close attention to the speaker.
- ✓ Watch the speaker's body language.
- ✓ Listen to the speaker's tone of voice.

**Don't:**
- ✓ Think about something else instead of listening.
- ✓ Ignore the listener to think about what you'll say next.
- ✓ Anticipate too quickly and jump to conclusions.
- ✓ Let what you think "twist" the speaker's words into something different from what he's really saying.

Mark these as **True** or **False**.

1. _____ Listening is just as important as speaking.

2. _____ You show good judgment when you decide in advance what someone is saying and then tune him out.

3. _____ Your ability to learn is improved when you use good listening skills.

4. _____ Poor eye contact may make the speaker think you aren't listening to what she's saying.

5. _____ Listening involves much more than just hearing the speaker's words.

6. _____ When the speaker pauses for a breath, it's a good time to jump in and say what you're thinking.

7. _____ It's okay to let your mind wander, as long as you return your attention to the speaker before he's finished.

8. _____ In the middle of a conversation, it's important that your comments relate to what the speaker is saying.

9. _____ Watching someone's eyes, body posture, and expressions can give you important information on how well he's listening to you.

# Conversation Skills—Get to the Point

When you're speaking with someone, get to the point and stay with the point you are trying to make. Leave out things that aren't important to include. After you've made your point, stop talking and don't ramble on.

Indicate whether each speaker **Rambles** or **Gets to the point**.

|  | **Rambles** | **Gets to the point** |  |
|---|---|---|---|
| 1. | _____ | _____ | I know it was last week that I went to the state fair. I know it because it was after I talked to you on the phone. The weather was nice, and the exhibits were interesting. I went to the state fair last year too. Have you ever gone to the state fair? Marge and I spent a lot of time at the exhibits last Tuesday. |
| 2. | _____ | _____ | Last night I watched a comedy show. It was really funny. The older daughter came home with her new husband, and they got together with each of their families. It was funny to watch them meet one another. |
| 3. | _____ | _____ | Last night I watched a comedy show. It was really funny. I liked it better than the one that came on just before it. The show has a new beginning now. It seems longer than the old one. I don't really know, but it was really funny to see the daughter come home with her new husband. Did you watch it? |
| 4. | _____ | _____ | I just returned from the grocery store. I saw Melvin in the parking lot. He was loading cartons into his trunk. I ate at the deli. Sara was there too. Then I went to the bank. |
| 5. | _____ | _____ | I just got back from doing errands. I'm exhausted. I went to the grocery store, ate at the deli, and then went to the bank. I like to get out and get things done, but sometimes it really wears me out. |

# Conversation Skills—Inclusion

Remember to include other people in conversations. To leave someone out can make that person feel like an outsider. Here are some things to help you include people in your conversations.

**Do:**
✓ Make an effort to reach out to everyone in the group.
✓ Be respectful of each person.
✓ Make eye contact with each person in the group.
✓ Be aware of each person's responses to what you say.

**Don't:**
✓ Ignore anyone in the group.
✓ Pay attention to only certain people in the group.
✓ Address your comments to only one person.

Are these speakers **Including** or **Excluding** others?

**Including**   **Excluding**

1. _____   _____   Come over here a minute so I can whisper something to you without anyone else hearing.

2. _____   _____   Let's ask George what he thinks about this problem.

3. _____   _____   How many of you have seen the new Harrison Ford movie?

4. _____   _____   Don't ask him. He never knows what he's talking about.

5. _____   _____   When I give a speech, I usually single out one person and talk directly to him. That way, I'm not as nervous.

6. _____   _____   Hold on a minute there, Myra. Nobody asked you for your opinion.

7. _____   _____   How many of you have had this same experience?

# Conversation Skills—Open Conversation

Being open to other opinions and viewpoints helps keep conversations going. Sometimes when we discuss something with others, we start to argue our position. Arguing can be destructive because it puts people on the defensive and stops discussion. Here are some *dos* and *don'ts* to keep conversations open.

**Do:**
- ✓ Stay on the subject.
- ✓ Be open to other people's viewpoints.
- ✓ Use a quiet voice.
- ✓ Focus on only the important facts.

**Don't:**
- ✓ Argue.
- ✓ Raise your voice.
- ✓ Reject other opinions without listening.

Are these speakers being **Open** or **Argumentative**?

| | **Open** | **Argumentative** | |
|---|---|---|---|
| 1. | _____ | _____ | As long as you're willing to listen to me, I'll hear you out. |
| 2. | _____ | _____ | I really don't want to fight about this, but you're being so unreasonable! |
| 3. | _____ | _____ | I think that was a pretty stupid remark. |
| 4. | _____ | _____ | Even though that upsets me, I'll think about what you said and get back to you. |
| 5. | _____ | _____ | No, I'm not going to listen to you because I don't think you know what you're talking about. |
| 6. | _____ | _____ | You've been doing some things lately that really bother me. Do you have some time to talk to me today? |
| 7. | _____ | _____ | You know, that was really an ignorant remark. |
| 8. | _____ | _____ | You sound like a broken record. Give it a break, okay? |

# Conversation Skills—Attentive Listeners

As a speaker, watch for signs that your listeners are paying attention to what you're saying.

**Do:**
✓ Watch for signs of attentiveness from your listeners.
✓ Look for signals of boredom or frustration.

**Don't:**
✓ Ignore sighs, yawns, fidgeting, or wandering eyes.
✓ Ramble on and on without letting other people speak.

Indicate whether these listeners are **Attentive** or **Bored**.

| | Attentive | Bored | |
|---|---|---|---|
| 1. | _____ | _____ | making good eye contact |
| 2. | _____ | _____ | fidgeting |
| 3. | _____ | _____ | sitting up straight, listening closely to what you're saying |
| 4. | _____ | _____ | trying not to yawn |
| 5. | _____ | _____ | rolling eyes |
| 6. | _____ | _____ | asking relevant questions in order to get you to say more |
| 7. | _____ | _____ | trying to break in and change the subject |
| 8. | _____ | _____ | calling someone else over to listen to the conversation too |
| 9. | _____ | _____ | nodding head frequently in agreement with you |
| 10. | _____ | _____ | gazing away, staring out the window |
| 11. | _____ | _____ | attempting to walk away |
| 12. | _____ | _____ | making hand gestures to encourage you to say more |

## Conversation Skills—Interruption

As a listener, be careful not to interrupt the speaker in the middle of what she is saying. When you interrupt, the speaker may feel that you believe her message isn't important. There are a few situations when it is appropriate to respectfully interrupt:

1. when the speaker is rambling on and on and losing her listeners
2. when the conversation is becoming offensive
3. when an emergency or safety issue arises
4. when another matter, such as a phone call, needs attention

Write **Do** or **Don't** to make each statement correct.

1. _____ interrupt if the speaker is making you late for an important appointment.

2. _____ interrupt by asking irrelevant questions.

3. _____ interrupt if you find the topic very uncomfortable.

4. _____ interrupt by finishing the speaker's sentences.

5. _____ interrupt to help tell a story.

6. _____ interrupt when someone is lying about your friend.

7. _____ interrupt to argue about unimportant details.

8. _____ interrupt if the building is on fire.

9. _____ interrupt to tell about the fish you caught last summer.

# Conversation Skills—Empathy

Be empathetic in conversations. Showing empathy means putting yourself in the place of another person so you can understand how he feels about the topic. Be sensitive to the people you're with and the mood they're in when bringing up topics to discuss. Religion, race, politics, or other subjects may be offensive to some people, so use tact when addressing these areas.

Indicate whether the speaker is **Tactful** or **Offensive**.

| | Tactful | Offensive | |
|---|---|---|---|
| 1. | _____ | _____ | You really worked hard and it was worth it! |
| 2. | _____ | _____ | Yuck! Get that disgusting food away from me! |
| 3. | _____ | _____ | I know someone who is much better looking than you. |
| 4. | _____ | _____ | Excuse me but your pants are ripped in the back. |
| 5. | _____ | _____ | You can't talk to my wife right now. She's busy! Don't bother us! |
| 6. | _____ | _____ | My son can't come to the phone right now. May I take a message? |
| 7. | _____ | _____ | I hope this gift is something I like. |
| 8. | _____ | _____ | Gee, where did you get that cheap-looking camera? |
| 9. | _____ | _____ | No, thank you. I'm really not interested right now. |
| 10. | _____ | _____ | I think you may have miscounted my change. |
| 11. | _____ | _____ | You cheated me out of some of my change! |

# Conversation Skills—Questions

Successful conversations need each person to be a speaker as well as a listener. By asking good questions, you can stimulate interesting conversation. How you word your questions will either keep a conversation going or stop discussion.

Questions that stimulate conversation usually require several words for an answer. They encourage an opinion or an explanation. For example:
*Why did you choose to live in this area?*
*How did you get into the kind of work you do?*

Questions that stop conversations are frequently questions that can be answered with "yes" or "no" or with only a few words. For example:
*Sure is a nice day, isn't it?*
*Where do you live?*
*What kind of work do you do?*

Indicate if these questions **Encourage** or **Stop** a conversation.

**Encourage**     **Stop**

1. _____ _____ What is your name?

2. _____ _____ Where did you last work?

3. _____ _____ Why do you say it's like working in a factory?

4. _____ _____ Why do you think cats are smarter than dogs?

5. _____ _____ What kind of dog do you have?

6. _____ _____ What happened on your vacation?

7. _____ _____ How do you think life will be different in 50 years?

8. _____ _____ When is your dentist appointment?

9. _____ _____ Do you like classical music?

10. _____ _____ How do you think classical music influenced rock and roll?

# Conversation Skills—Sensitivity

There are certain times when it isn't a good idea to begin a conversation. Be careful to choose the right time to talk about touchy or serious topics. Be sensitive to other people's moods when starting conversations.

What are five topics you wouldn't bring up to a family member when she is tired or upset?

1. _____
2. _____
3. _____
4. _____
5. _____

Mark these situations as good times to **Start** a conversation or to **Wait** before beginning a conversation.

| | **Start** | **Wait** | |
|---|---|---|---|
| 1. | _____ | _____ | Your spouse just got home from a very tiring day at work. |
| 2. | _____ | _____ | Your spouse has had time to relax and unwind after a long day. |
| 3. | _____ | _____ | You're having a leisurely lunch with a close friend. |
| 4. | _____ | _____ | You and your family are beginning a long car trip. |
| 5. | _____ | _____ | At the end of a long drive, you're tired and have gotten lost several times. |
| 6. | _____ | _____ | You're late for an important appointment. |

# Idioms and Proverbs

Being able to interpret information literally and abstractly is necessary for effective verbal reasoning. Someone who has had a change in his brain function will have the tendency to interpret and explain everything in concrete, literal, here-and-now terms. He will have difficulty understanding how sentence meaning changes with the use of abstract words and concepts.

Providing practice with idioms and proverbs will assist your client in being able to recognize when something is literal or abstract. It will increase his awareness that there are two levels of meaning and help him to see how those different levels can change a conversation or situation.

For all of the tasks in this section, it is recommended that you have your client explain what the idiom or proverb means. There will be times when he will interpret an expression by using situations instead of explaining the actual meaning of the idiom or proverb. This strategy should be encouraged as it uses the natural tendency of applying abstract meaning to real situations in life. For example, when interpreting *While the cat's away, the mice will play*, your client may say, "When the boss isn't around, the workers slack off."

# Expression Completion and Explanation

Complete the expression. Then explain what it means.

1. An apple a day _____.

2. A penny saved _____.

3. Time heals _____.

4. A fool and his money _____.

5. A bird in the hand _____.

6. The grass is always greener _____.

7. You can't see the forest _____.

8. Honesty is _____.

9. Blood is thicker _____.

10. There is more than one way to _____.

11. Absence makes the _____.

12. A friend in need is _____.

13. Fools rush in where _____.

14. Don't count your chickens _____.

15. He put his foot in _____.

16. The love of money is _____.

17. Don't judge a book _____.

18. Too many cooks _____.

19. Early to bed and early to rise makes _____.

20. Don't put all your eggs _____.

# Expression Completion and Explanation

Complete the expression. Then explain what it means.

1. You can't have your cake and _____.

2. Look before _____.

3. You can't teach an old dog _____.

4. It's like looking for a needle _____.

5. Haste makes _____.

6. Silence is _____.

7. He is a jack of _____.

8. Two heads are _____.

9. You can't get blood _____.

10. Every cloud has _____.

11. Better late _____.

12. Birds of a feather _____.

13. Don't cry over _____.

14. Curiosity killed _____.

15. When the cat's away, _____.

16. Don't kill the goose that lays _____.

17. Beggars should not _____.

18. He who laughs last, _____.

19. Don't make a mountain _____.

20. Actions speak _____.

# Missing Letters

Determine the letter that is missing from each of the following expressions. Write the complete expression on the line. Then explain what it means.

> **Example:** Insert the letter E into Bttrlatthannvr to form *Better late than never*.

1. jckofllltrdes _____

2. Afrindinndisafrindindd _____

3. chipfftheldblck _____

4. Tmewlltell _____

5. Whrthr'sawillthr'saway _____

6. Tmanycksspilthebrth _____

7. woheadsarebeerhanone _____

8. Asttchntmesavesnne _____

9. Twwrngsdn'tmakearight _____

10. Rllingstnesgathernmss _____

11. Ncssityisthmothrofallinvntion _____

12. Aflandhismneyaresnparted _____

13. Youcn'thveyourckendetittoo _____

14. can'seeheforesforherees _____

15. Thrarothrfishinthsa _____

# Mixed-Up Expressions

Each expression contains a part of the body. The body parts have been mixed up. Write the correct answers on the lines. The first one is done as an example. Then explain what each expression means.

1. You made it by the skin of your leg.          teeth

2. It's on the tip of my chest.          _____

3. I have butterflies in my nose.          _____

4. Get it off your tongue.          _____

5. She pulled the wool over his foot.          _____

6. You're pulling my teeth.          _____

7. It's right under your head.          _____

8. Now the shoe is on the other stomach.          _____

9. Off the top of my eyes, I will guess, "25."          _____

10. He has a chip on his head.          _____

11. Lay your elbow on my shoulder.          _____

12. It may leave a bad taste in your face.          _____

13. Keep a straight shoulder.          _____

14. Give me more stomach room.          _____

15. Your eyes are bigger than your mouth.          _____

# Expression Interpretation—Literal and Abstract

Write the literal meaning and the abstract meaning for each expression. The first one is done as an example.

| Idiom | Literal | Abstract |
|---|---|---|
| 1. He has a green thumb. | His thumb is the color green. | He's good at growing plants. |
| 2. She has a frog in her throat. | | |
| 3. That's not my cup of tea. | | |
| 4. He killed two birds with one stone. | | |
| 5. Let sleeping dogs lie. | | |
| 6. Her husband is a back-seat driver. | | |

# Expression Interpretation—Literal and Abstract

Write the literal meaning and the abstract meaning for each expression. The first one is done as an example.

| Idiom | Literal | Abstract |
|---|---|---|
| 1. It's raining cats and dogs. | Dogs and cats are falling out of the sky. | It's raining very hard. |
| 2. You should get it off your chest. | | |
| 3. She had him wrapped around her little finger. | | |
| 4. He has a chip on his shoulder. | | |
| 5. She should bury the hatchet. | | |
| 6. His eyes were bigger than his stomach. | | |

# Expression Interpretation—Literal and Abstract

Write the literal meaning and the abstract meaning for each expression. The first one is done as an example.

| Idiom | Literal | Abstract |
|---|---|---|
| 1. Every cloud has a silver lining. | Clouds have a lining made of silver. | There are good things in every situation. |
| 2. All that glitters is not gold. | | |
| 3. There's more than one way to skin a cat. | | |
| 4. An apple a day keeps the doctor away. | | |
| 5. The grass is always greener on the other side of the fence. | | |
| 6. You can't teach an old dog new tricks. | | |

# Matching Proverbs to Situations

Match each proverb to its situation.

_____ 1. While the cat's away, the mice will play.

_____ 2. Don't judge a book by its cover.

_____ 3. An apple a day keeps the doctor away.

_____ 4. Time flies.

_____ 5. All that glitters is not gold.

_____ 6. Look before you leap.

_____ 7. A friend in need is a friend indeed.

_____ 8. Don't put all your eggs in one basket.

_____ 9. Don't count your chickens before they're hatched.

_____ 10. Honesty is the best policy.

_____ 11. Too many cooks spoil the broth.

_____ 12. When in Rome, do as the Romans do.

a. Winning the lottery didn't make them any happier.

b. When she heard of the tragedy, she immediately went over to see what she could do to help.

c. She was so sure about the new job that she went out and bought new clothes.

d. The workers took it easy when their supervisor went on a business trip.

e. They never solved anything because everyone thought his opinion was the most important.

f. When she visited Haiti, she wore a skirt every day, just like the women who lived there.

g. She cooked balanced meals so her family would stay healthy.

h. The company investigated every aspect of the deal before committing themselves.

i. The broken-down piece of furniture was really a valuable antique.

j. He decided to tell his neighbor that he broke the window.

k. The meeting was over before all of the decisions could be made.

l. He invested his money in several different ventures.

# Categorization

Being able to identify and label categories is another key element in effective verbal reasoning. The tasks in this section begin with naming objects that belong to a category with the added element of quantifying directions to help your client zero in on more specific category members. This will aid in your client's ability to reason verbally within given parameters. Tasks progress to describing and comparing characteristics of objects to help your client present salient information in an organized, complete manner. Tasks continue with your client determining what the main category is among given items and determining which of the items does not belong with the others. This will aid in your client's ability to verbally reason using inclusion and exclusion principles.

The tasks then progress to a level which incorporates a more refined categorization method. Your client is presented with tasks that require him to provide a general category, a subcategory, and a specific member. These tasks teach the subtleties of categorization and are actually reflective of the skills we use daily. This also gives your client practice solving a task from multiple directions, thus helping him establish the process for using flexible verbal reasoning when problem solving.

Once your client's skills are established at the word level, the tasks progress to the sentence level. This is a functional task as it is reflective of communication or of the process we use when completing familiar tasks. For example, when you are looking for a new car, you must determine what make of car you want, then the model, and finally the specific features you want that model to have. The sentence tasks give your client practice with this kind of categorizing which involves a significant verbal reasoning element.

# Naming Objects by Attributes

Answer the following questions. There may be more than one correct answer.

1. What object is usually black?
2. What object is large but not alive?
3. What beverage can be hot or cold?
4. What costs more than five thousand dollars?
5. What can be green or red?
6. What can be bounced or rolled?
7. What would you find in the city as well as in the country?
8. What object is expected to pop?
9. What breaks when it is bent?
10. What can move fast or slow?
11. What can be short or tall?
12. What needs to be cut because it grows?
13. What can see better at night than during the day?
14. What becomes slippery when it is wet?
15. What improves with age?
16. What can be noisy or quiet?
17. What can float or sink?
18. What needs water to exist?
19. What expires on a yearly basis?
20. What is cooked and then eaten cold?

# Naming Objects by Attributes

Answer the following questions. There may be more than one correct answer.

1. What can be short or long?
2. What is rectangular and large?
3. What can bend but does not break?
4. What is made of metal and rubber?
5. What is cold and slippery?
6. What is small but expensive?
7. What is large but inexpensive?
8. What can a person see better at night than during the day?
9. What can be red, green, or yellow?
10. What can be sharp or dull?
11. What can fly but cannot walk?
12. What has four corners?
13. What can be permanent or temporary?
14. What can be made of wood or metal?
15. What can people see through?
16. What is smaller than it was ten years ago?
17. What lives longer than a human being?
18. What sleeps more than it is awake?
19. What can live in water as well as on land?
20. What can go up and down as well as left and right?

# Naming Objects by Attributes

Answer the following questions. There may be more than one correct answer.

1. What can fly or walk?
2. What can be made of plastic or cloth?
3. What can melt or freeze?
4. What can be light or heavy?
5. What needs sunlight to exist?
6. What stretches when you pull on it?
7. What takes several people to accomplish?
8. What costs less than five dollars?
9. What needs to be wet before you can use it?
10. What can be bright or dark?
11. What can be parted?
12. What can be white or black?
13. What can you put in a pocket?
14. What is solid but floats?
15. What is round and hollow?
16. What can be bottled or canned?
17. What needs food to exist?
18. What needs to run on electricity?
19. What can be done better by a child than by an adult?
20. What can be done better by an adult than by a child?

## Description—One Object

Describe the characteristics of a car. Some of the features listed may not apply.

Object: **car**

1. height _____

2. weight _____

3. length _____

4. width _____

5. color _____

6. durability _____

7. materials _____

8. shape _____

9. size _____

10. texture _____

11. density _____

12. temperature _____

13. value _____

14. function _____

15. other uses _____

# Description—One Object

Describe the characteristics of an object you choose or someone else chooses. Some of the features may not apply.

Object: _____

1. height _____

2. weight _____

3. length _____

4. width _____

5. color _____

6. durability _____

7. materials _____

8. shape _____

9. size _____

10. texture _____

11. density _____

12. temperature _____

13. value _____

14. function _____

15. other uses _____

# Description and Comparison—Two Objects

Describe the characteristics of a bicycle and an airplane. Then state how they are similar and different. Some of the features may not apply.

| | bicycle | airplane |
|---|---|---|
| 1. height | | |
| 2. weight | | |
| 3. length | | |
| 4. width | | |
| 5. color | | |
| 6. durability | | |
| 7. materials | | |
| 8. shape | | |
| 9. size | | |
| 10. texture | | |
| 11. density | | |
| 12. temperature | | |
| 13. value | | |
| 14. function | | |
| 15. other uses | | |

# Description and Comparison—Two Objects

Describe the characteristics of two objects you choose or someone else chooses. Some of the features may not apply.

| | Object 1 | Object 2 |
|---|---|---|
| 1. height | | |
| 2. weight | | |
| 3. length | | |
| 4. width | | |
| 5. color | | |
| 6. durability | | |
| 7. materials | | |
| 8. shape | | |
| 9. size | | |
| 10. texture | | |
| 11. density | | |
| 12. temperature | | |
| 13. value | | |
| 14. function | | |
| 15. other uses | | |

# Which Does Not Belong?

Mark the word in each row that does not belong with the others.

1. beautiful — pretty — plain — attractive — good looking
2. scrawny — sticky — bony — skinny — thin
3. glimmer — flicker — reduce — sparkle — glitter
4. spiral — walk — run — trot — gallop
5. investigate — explore — research — delve — limit
6. height — length — width — ruler — weight
7. fighting — docile — meek — humble — submissive
8. punish — theorize — penalize — discipline — correct
9. society — association — alliance — voice — group
10. enormous — huge — large — big — question
11. false — inaccurate — shocking — fraudulent — fake
12. pity — compassion — mercy — jealousy — sympathy
13. hunt — attend — pursue — chase — search
14. home — domicile — house — residence — basement
15. computer — cell phone — pyramid — DVD player — digital camera
16. awful — good — great — wonderful — fantastic
17. math — athletics — gymnastics — calisthenics — acrobatics
18. smile — grin — chuckle — whine — laugh
19. hour — minute — second — day — schedule
20. tree — dirt — plant — flower — bush

# Which Does Not Belong?

Mark the word in each row that does not belong with the others.

| | | | | | |
|---|---|---|---|---|---|
| 1. | joke | guarantee | warranty | assurance | promise |
| 2. | plate | dish | glass | oven | silverware |
| 3. | whim | what | where | when | why |
| 4. | remember | recall | retain | recollect | return |
| 5. | pious | devout | religious | impish | faithful |
| 6. | slow | fast | quick | rapid | speedy |
| 7. | stocks | IRAs | bonds | money market | show |
| 8. | glory | splendor | horror | grandeur | magnificence |
| 9. | synthesize | make | imagine | construct | build |
| 10. | purr | bark | meow | quack | snap |
| 11. | frank | disgusted | sincere | honest | candid |
| 12. | circle | curved | square | oval | round |
| 13. | draw | fight | brawl | wrestle | combat |
| 14. | vacate | wait | leave | exit | depart |
| 15. | greetings | hello | hi | welcome | visitation |
| 16. | song | melody | book | music | tone |
| 17. | silver | mug | cup | glass | goblet |
| 18. | reduce | lower | lessen | increase | cheapen |
| 19. | supple | steel | flexible | pliable | yielding |
| 20. | tax | toll | levy | ticket | duty |

# General Category Labeling

Name the general category. The first one is done for you.

1. _____furniture_____ chair, rocker

2. _____ guard dogs, German shepherd

3. _____ stuffed animals, teddy bears

4. _____ apples, Macintosh

5. _____ game shows, Jeopardy

6. _____ green, olive

7. _____ house, split-level

8. _____ evergreen, spruce

9. _____ sweater, cardigan

10. _____ water vehicle, ship

11. _____ shoes, loafers

12. _____ organ, heart

13. _____ woodwinds, clarinet

14. _____ spoons, teaspoon

15. _____ wild animals, bear

# Subcategory Labeling

Name an item that is more general than the word on the right, but more specific than the word on the left. The first one is done for you.

1. solar system _____ planet _____ Jupiter
2. sweets _____ Hershey Bar
3. appliances _____ coffee maker
4. clothing _____ jeans
5. sports _____ balance beam
6. color _____ yellow
7. weather _____ drizzle
8. vegetables _____ lima
9. animals _____ wolf
10. furniture _____ coffee table
11. entertainment _____ "The Phantom of the Opera"
12. body parts _____ nose
13. medicines _____ aspirin
14. instruments _____ trumpet
15. accessories _____ necklace

# Specific Member Labeling

Name a specific category member for each set of words. The first one is done for you.

1. felines, cats, _____Siamese_____

2. drinks, cold beverages, _____

3. things that sting, stinging insects, _____

4. seasonings, spice, _____

5. stone, gemstone, _____

6. sports equipment, tennis equipment, _____

7. animals, domestic pets, _____

8. movies, musical movies, _____

9. footwear, shoes, _____

10. time, seasons, _____

11. emotions, positive feelings, _____

12. cars, foreign-made cars, _____

13. milk products, cheese, _____

14. vehicles, emergency vehicles, _____

15. plants, weeds, _____

# Categorization Grid

Fill in the chart with the appropriate information. The first one is done for you.

| General Category | Subcategory | Specific Member |
|---|---|---|
| professions | medical professions | **nurse** |
| transportation | motorized transportation | |
| | dogs | poodle |
| appliances | | electric can opener |
| | books | *Treasure Island* |
| clothing | | jacket |
| | eagles | bald eagle |
| stores | department stores | |
| | blue | navy blue |
| precipitation | | drizzle |
| sports | | skiing |
| | pens | felt-tip pens |

# Categorization Grid

Fill in the chart with the appropriate information. The first one is done for you.

| General Category | Subcategory | Specific Member |
|---|---|---|
| entertainment | musicals | *My Fair Lady* |
| plants | | dandelion |
| | leafy greens | lettuce |
| birds | water fowl | |
| | limbs | legs |
| tools | | hoe |
| illnesses | childhood illnesses | |
| | winter sports | ice hockey |
| medicine | cold medicine | |
| | dairy products | milk |
| | television news | *60 Minutes* |
| solar system | planets | |

# Categorization in Sentences

Underline the general category, subcategory, and specific member within each sentence. The first one is done for you.

1. In science, we studied the <u>solar system</u>, particularly the <u>planet</u> <u>Mars</u>.

2. My favorite animal in the zoo's bear exhibit is the polar bear.

3. The medical profession recommends that you see your doctor once a year, including your podiatrist.

4. There were so many cheeses in the dairy section of the store, I had trouble deciding on the extra-sharp cheddar.

5. When it comes to toys, Sammy likes construction toys, especially Lincoln Logs.

6. When I go to a dog show, I enjoy watching Labrador retrievers and other dogs in the sporting dogs division.

7. She finally chose *Gone With the Wind* from all the novels in the literature section of the library.

8. With all of today's means of transportation, I prefer to travel by air transportation in a jet.

9. When we were looking for a vacation spot, I got literature on national parks before deciding on Yellowstone.

10. After looking at many flowers, I bought tulips and other spring bloomers.

11. I find playing *Search the Mountain* video game an excellent form of entertainment.

12. The furniture builder made chairs, specializing in rocking chairs.

# Convergent Reasoning

When verbally reasoning, a person must frequently take multiple pieces of information, comprehend them, mentally manipulate them, and then integrate them with information already present in his cognitive knowledge in order to converge upon the specific, logical response.

This section provides a variety of tasks to give your client multiple opportunities to improve his convergent reasoning abilities. The varied formats provide change for your client so he does not become habituated to a specific process or become bored with using the same format over and over again while retraining his convergent reasoning skills.

It is important that your client feels some enjoyment and challenge when working with these tasks. There will be some tasks a client enjoys doing more than others. If this is the case, just use the tasks your client enjoys as he will be more interested in completing them.

Convergent reasoning involves many different kinds of skills. For some of the tasks (e.g. negative true/false statements), it involves thinking in reverse of the normal process used for answering questions. Other tasks involve an abstract element that needs to be determined in order to answer the questions (e.g., *Diagrams with Choices*). The deduction puzzles require multiple abilities, such as being able to integrate one clue with another, being able to use exclusion principles to eliminate possible answers, and using the grid to give information for determining a possible response. All of these elements are important for successful verbal reasoning.

# Fact/Opinion

Determine if the statements are facts or opinions. A fact can generally be proven. An opinion can be debated or argued about. (Hint: Be careful! You are not to determine if these statements are true or false.)

Write an **F** if the statement is a fact. Write an **O** if the statement is an opinion.

1. \_\_\_\_ Watching too much television can be harmful to a person.

2. \_\_\_\_ Watching the TV news can help a person learn about the world.

3. \_\_\_\_ Many people watch TV to help pass the time.

4. \_\_\_\_ An all-movie channel is better to watch than an all-sports channel.

5. \_\_\_\_ There are many different cable channels.

6. \_\_\_\_ Many reruns of old shows are more entertaining than new shows.

7. \_\_\_\_ Cartoons are only for children to watch.

8. \_\_\_\_ Many children watch cartoons on Saturday mornings.

9. \_\_\_\_ Shows in color are better than shows in black and white.

10. \_\_\_\_ Sometimes shows are pre-empted because of important news reports.

11. \_\_\_\_ You can use a remote control to change channels.

12. \_\_\_\_ Soap operas are true-to-life situations.

13. \_\_\_\_ The History Channel is more educational than the Court Channel.

14. \_\_\_\_ It is possible to record shows to watch later.

15. \_\_\_\_ Children should not be allowed to watch all shows.

# Fact/Opinion

Determine if the statements are facts or opinions. A fact can generally be proven. An opinion can be debated or argued about. (Hint: Be careful! You are not to determine if these statements are true or false.)

Write an **F** if the statement is a fact. Write an **O** if the statement is an opinion.

1. \_\_\_\_ Cats are better pets than dogs.

2. \_\_\_\_ Some people prefer to own cats.

3. \_\_\_\_ A dog can be taught tricks.

4. \_\_\_\_ A dog is a better companion than a cat.

5. \_\_\_\_ A cat loses too much hair around the house.

6. \_\_\_\_ A cat has a rough tongue.

7. \_\_\_\_ Dogs are easier to take care of than cats.

8. \_\_\_\_ Many dogs are bigger than cats.

9. \_\_\_\_ Many cats catch mice.

10. \_\_\_\_ Cats should be allowed to go outside.

11. \_\_\_\_ A large dog should not be kept in an apartment.

12. \_\_\_\_ Many cats like catnip.

13. \_\_\_\_ A dog should be walked at least one mile a day.

14. \_\_\_\_ Many dogs like to chew on bones.

15. \_\_\_\_ A cat should have its front claws removed.

# Negative True/False Statements

Write **T** if the statement is true. Write **F** is the statement is false. As these are negative true/false statements, they are tricky. Take your time and think about them.

1. \_\_\_\_ Coffee is not a hot drink.

2. \_\_\_\_ Coats are not something to wear when it is a sizzling hot day.

3. \_\_\_\_ A dog is not an animal that barks.

4. \_\_\_\_ Trucks are not toys that children play with.

5. \_\_\_\_ A horn is not something loud that can be beeped.

6. \_\_\_\_ A saw is not a tool you sand with.

7. \_\_\_\_ A florist is not a person who butchers meat.

8. \_\_\_\_ Fires are not something hot that burn.

9. \_\_\_\_ A sink is not something in your bureau drawer.

10. \_\_\_\_ An ice-cream cone is not something to lick.

11. \_\_\_\_ Cola is not something fizzy to drink.

12. \_\_\_\_ A light is not something bright to turn on in the dark.

13. \_\_\_\_ A wallet is not something made of leather to wear.

14. \_\_\_\_ Sneakers do not have soles.

15. \_\_\_\_ Trees do not have hands.

16. \_\_\_\_ Pans are not something made of plastic.

17. \_\_\_\_ Cats are not animals with sharp claws.

18. \_\_\_\_ An alarm is not something noisy used for driving a car.

19. \_\_\_\_ A table is not a piece of furniture.

20. \_\_\_\_ Water does not always put out a grease fire.

# Negative True/False Statements

Write **T** if the statement is true. Write **F** is the statement is false. As these are negative true/false statements, they are tricky. Take your time and think about them.

1. \_\_\_\_ An apple does not have seeds.

2. \_\_\_\_ A chair is not a utensil used for cooking.

3. \_\_\_\_ Maple trees do not lose their leaves in the spring.

4. \_\_\_\_ Bricks are not a material used for building walls.

5. \_\_\_\_ A mop is not a thing used for cleaning windows.

6. \_\_\_\_ A sweatshirt is not an article of clothing to make you warmer.

7. \_\_\_\_ Most plants do not need water and sunlight to grow.

8. \_\_\_\_ Pink is not a color that is dark.

9. \_\_\_\_ Socks are not clothing worn on the feet.

10. \_\_\_\_ A bowling ball does not bounce as high as a basketball.

11. \_\_\_\_ A student has not yet graduated from school.

12. \_\_\_\_ Lawn chairs are not used outside in the summer.

13. \_\_\_\_ A fence is a not a wooden structure used inside of the house.

14. \_\_\_\_ A television is not an appliance used for cleaning.

15. \_\_\_\_ Barbecue grills are not used for cooking meat.

16. \_\_\_\_ Smiling is not a facial expression that shows displeasure.

17. \_\_\_\_ Glasses are not worn to help one's hearing.

18. \_\_\_\_ Grass is not a plant that grows in the lawn.

19. \_\_\_\_ Wood is not used for burning in a fire.

20. \_\_\_\_ A cat is not a pet that can fly.

## Sequencing

Rearrange each group of words so their meanings progress in degree or occurrence.

> **Example:** *hot, boiling, lukewarm* should be rearranged to *lukewarm, hot, boiling*

1. Tuesday, Sunday, Friday _____
2. yesterday, tomorrow, today _____
3. hour, minute, second _____
4. year, century, decade _____
5. pay, order, eat _____
6. depart, pack, arrive _____
7. junior high, kindergarten, high school _____
8. butterfly, cocoon, caterpillar _____
9. play, shuffle, win, deal _____
10. blossom, seed, bud, sprout _____
11. catch, bait, cast, clean _____
12. search, lose, find _____
13. read, test, memorize _____
14. August, January, October, May _____
15. plan, occupy, build, dream _____

# Sequencing

Rearrange each group of words so their meanings progress in degree.

> **Example:** *hot, boiling, lukewarm* should be rearranged to *lukewarm, hot, boiling*

1. freezing, cool, cold _____
2. grandmother, daughter, mother _____
3. sprint, walk, jog _____
4. most, least, more, less _____
5. glance, stare, look _____
6. cry, whimper, sob _____
7. medium, well-done, rare _____
8. boil, warm, simmer _____
9. furious, angry, bothered _____
10. private, general, sergeant _____
11. quiet, silent, loud _____
12. positive, negative, neutral _____
13. middle, lower, upper _____
14. convict, suspect, investigate _____
15. giant, large, tiny, small _____

# Sequencing

Rearrange each group of words so their meanings progress in degree.

> **Example:** *hot, boiling, lukewarm* should be rearranged to *lukewarm, hot, boiling*

1. shout, whisper, silence, talk _____
2. grin, giggle, guffaw, laugh _____
3. mansion, house, cabin, shed _____
4. brilliant, dim, dark, bright _____
5. farther, far, near, farthest _____
6. flow, gush, trickle, drop _____
7. governor, president, mayor _____
8. sad, joyous, glad, content _____
9. continent, town, nation, state _____
10. hideous, plain, pretty, ugly _____
11. ancient, futuristic, present, old _____
12. impossible, possible, definite, probable _____
13. feast, fast, meal, snack _____
14. black, ivory, white, gray _____
15. minute, small, large, medium _____

# Increasing Word Length

Add a letter or letters to the beginning or end of the second word to form a new word.

> **Examples:** no, not, <u>note</u>    sure, assure, <u>assuredly</u>

1. I, in, _____
2. ace, race, _____
3. ten, tend, _____
4. at, hat, _____
5. am, cream, _____
6. at, oat, _____
7. tar, star, _____
8. act, tact, _____
9. us, use, _____
10. an, van, _____
11. rag, drag, _____
12. on, don, _____
13. ace, pace, _____
14. row, grow, _____
15. on, one, _____
16. hot, shot, _____
17. old, cold, _____
18. ice, lice, _____
19. pa, pan, _____
20. it, item, _____
21. ouch, touch, _____
22. an, hang, _____
23. me, meet, _____
24. am, came, _____
25. an, rank, _____
26. ever, every, _____
27. aid, maid, _____
28. hang, change, _____
29. art, part, _____
30. am, dam, _____

## Diagrams with Choices

Match each phrase with the diagram that illustrates it.

> **Example:** VISION   VISION = <u>double vision</u>

1. four-leaf clover

       C
       A
       L
       M

2. down in the dumps

   TROUBLE   TROUBLE

3. broken promise

   PIECE
   PIECE  SUIT
   PIECE

4. split hairs

   IIIII  RIGHT  IIIII

   PRO ⚡ MISE

5. three-piece suit

   HA
     IRS

6. double trouble

   DUMPS  DOWN  DUMPS
       DUMPS  DUMPS

7. calm down

8. right between the eyes

   LEAF
   LEAF
   LEAF  CLOVER
   LEAF

# Diagrams with Choices

Match each phrase with the diagram that illustrates it.

> **Example:** VISION   VISION   =   <u>double vision</u>

1. splitting headache

2. chip on his shoulder

3. all over with

4. rock around the clock

5. small world

6. broken heart

7. blank slate

8. six of one and half a dozen of another

 

one   another
one   another
one   another
one   another
one   another
one   another

HE ⚡ ART

_____ SLATE

world

CHIP
HIS SHOULDER

HEAD<sub>ACHE</sub>

$\dfrac{\text{ALL}}{\text{WITH}}$

     R
K  CLOCK  O
     C

# Diagrams with Choices

Match each phrase with the diagram that illustrates it.

> **Example:**  VISION   VISION  =  <u>double vision</u>

1. three-ring circus

    **DEAL**

2. big deal

    $$\frac{EGGS}{EASY}$$

3. eggs over easy

    ⟵ OVER

4. leftover

    shooter
    shooter
    shooter
    shooter
    shooter
    shooter

5. six-shooter

    KCABBACK

6. stationed overseas

    $$\frac{STATIONED}{SEAS}$$

7. be on time

    TBEME / TIME (BE above TIME)

8. back to back

    RING
    RING      CIRCUS
    RING

---

*Verbal Reasoning—Convergent Reasoning*

# Diagrams Without Choices

What common expression do each of these diagrams represent? The blank lines tell you how many words are in the answer.

|R|E|A|D|

_____ _____
_____ _____

```
E
L    safety      _____ _____
K    safety      _____ _____
C    safety
U    safety
B
```

```
give    get    _____
give    get    _____
give    get    _____
give    get
```

DOfootOR    _____ _____
            _____ _____

DNAH    _____

stand    __ _____
  I

wear    _____ _____
long

cycle
cycle    _____
cycle

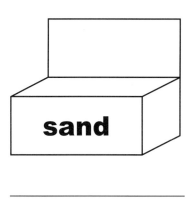

_____

school    _____ _____

_____ _____

*Verbal Reasoning—Convergent Reasoning*
*WALC 9: Verbal and Visual Reasoning*

# Diagrams Without Choices

What common expression do each of these diagrams represent? The blank lines tell you how many words are in the answer.

S
T
A
I
R
S

_____

R
O
R O A D S  _____
D
S

_____ ✓

**Wish**

____ ____

MIDmonkeyDLE

_____  ____  _____  _____

CEN
   T  _____ ____
   U
   R  _____ _____
   Y

 ship   _____
CCCCCC
       _____

T
E
S  _____

LE  _____
  VEL  _____

| meal | meal | meal |

____ ____ _____

# Anagrams

Rearrange the letters in each word to form a different word.

> **Example:** item = <u>time</u>

1. late  _____
2. gape  _____
3. meat  _____
4. pleat  _____
5. grab  _____
6. veer  _____
7. peat  _____
8. fare  _____
9. gods  _____
10. life  _____
11. tea  _____
12. from  _____
13. race  _____
14. seat  _____
15. note  _____
16. pier  _____
17. mane  _____
18. bleat  _____
19. tops  _____
20. sewn  _____
21. filed  _____
22. aide  _____
23. dire  _____
24. charm  _____
25. reef  _____
26. shore  _____
27. sire  _____
28. ends  _____
29. bore  _____
30. rite  _____

# Anagrams

Rearrange the letters in each word to form a different word.

> **Example:** item = <u>time</u>

1. lime _____
2. slate _____
3. kits _____
4. space _____
5. fate _____
6. mace _____
7. night _____
8. rage _____
9. lead _____
10. sole _____
11. cafe _____
12. lure _____
13. mothers _____
14. thorn _____
15. tide _____
16. dad _____
17. moor _____
18. tear _____
19. rues _____
20. peach _____
21. sheet _____
22. stage _____
23. ward _____
24. paste _____
25. tarp _____
26. cape _____
27. bread _____
28. peon _____
29. skate _____
30. cheat _____

# Anagrams in Sentences

Rearrange the letters of each underlined word to form a new word. Then use it to complete each sentence.

> **Example:** There was an <u>odor</u> coming from under the <u>door</u>.

1. Please do only one <u>item</u> at a _____.

2. The <u>tarps</u> will cover the _____ that need protection.

3. The man with the <u>beard</u> is buttering his _____.

4. Do you want to <u>eat</u> or have _____?

5. It was <u>cheap</u> to buy this _____ at the roadside stand.

6. Take <u>care</u> when you run the _____ in New York City.

7. She bumped the <u>lamp</u> with her _____.

8. It <u>takes</u> practice to learn how to _____.

9. The instructors <u>teach</u> children not to _____ on tests.

10. The <u>thorn</u> bushes were in the _____ part of the garden.

11. The <u>last</u> ingredient you should add is _____.

12. I'm in <u>dire</u> need of a _____.

13. The members on the football <u>team</u> eat _____ before every game.

14. Dan's <u>seat</u> was on the _____ side of the stadium.

15. Get the <u>form</u> _____ the receptionist.

# Anagrams in Sentences

Rearrange the letters of each underlined word to form a new word. Then use it to complete each sentence.

> **Example:** There was an <u>odor</u> coming from under the <u>door</u>.

1. The dolphins swam <u>free</u> through the coral _____.

2. His <u>horse</u> loved to run along the _____.

3. He got an excellent <u>deal</u> on some _____ pipes.

4. Put <u>these</u> pillowcases on after you put on the _____.

5. You can <u>stop</u> after you dry the _____ and pans.

6. She dropped her <u>brush</u> in the _____ beside the porch.

7. Do you know what <u>thing</u> made all that noise last _____?

8. He flew into a <u>rage</u> when he couldn't get his car into third _____.

9. "Listen, <u>chum</u>, I can't take _____ more of this!"

10. The <u>bore</u> wore his _____ around the house all day.

11. You should <u>name</u> your horse after the color of his _____.

12. The president's <u>aide</u> came up with a brilliant _____.

13. I <u>fear</u> that I can't afford the plane _____.

14. The <u>recipe</u> stated that you shouldn't _____ the crust with a knife.

15. It took the teacher <u>quite</u> a while to _____ the class.

# Symbol Substitution

Choose a symbol to complete each word below. Spell out the word the symbol represents in the blank.

> **Example:**  & means *and*     h _&___ = h _and___

|   |   |   |   |
|---|---|---|---|
| • | x | , | + |
| : | = | % | & |
| ♥ | ★ | π | ¢ |

1. _____y

2. _____ical

3. _____ndment

4. sweet_____

5. _____age

6. _____ity

7. sur_____

8. b_____age

9. _____er

10. _____board

11. _____nt

12. _____ Square

*Verbal Reasoning—Convergent Reasoning*
*WALC 9: Verbal and Visual Reasoning*

# Symbol Substitution

Choose a symbol to complete each word below. Spell out the word the symbol represents in the blank.

> **Example:** & means *and*    h &___ = h *and*

|   |   |   |   |
|---|---|---|---|
| • | x | , | + |
| : | = | % | & |
| ♥ | ★ | π | ¢ |

1. _____ch

2. _____ile

3. _____nch

4. _____ial

5. _____h

6. _____burn

7. _____ipede

8. _____nder

9. _____ic

10. _____roid

11. _____ly

12. New York _____

# Change One Letter

Change one letter in each of the words in a group to get three new words that are members of the same category.

> **Example:** bit, wall, globe = bat, ball, glove

1. grange, greet, mellow = _____
2. hold, salver, copter = _____
3. torn, pets, bumpkin = _____
4. touch, choir, sable = _____
5. yeah, sour, mouth = _____
6. liver, cheek, golf = _____
7. boot, setter, nose = _____
8. short, packet, stacks = _____
9. shot, boat, skipper = _____
10. stake, hurtle, told = _____
11. mink, sofa, ten = _____
12. log, can, wish = _____
13. aim, soot, angle = _____
14. mouth, say, leek = _____
15. ore, hive, forth = _____

# Change One Letter

Change one letter in each of the words in a group to get three new words that are members of the same category.

▶ **Example:** bit, wall, globe = bat, ball, glove

1. line, cheery, gripe = _____

2. crush, come, hurlers = _____

3. clue, tale, stable = _____

4. trick, cur, ran = _____

5. brunch, swig, stock = _____

6. grain, plate, but = _____

7. halt, popper, glove = _____

8. torch, heat, small = _____

9. tick, sail, belt = _____

10. food, leg, stack = _____

11. gulf, crack, liking = _____

12. fate, deck, thin = _____

13. fowl, dash, class = _____

14. dour, well, flour = _____

15. main, hall, show = _____

# Change One Letter—Create

Now it's time to create some of your own word puzzles. Use three words that belong to the same category. Change one letter in each word. Make sure the new words are actual words. Remember to use common categories.

Here are three examples:

| orange | = | grange |
|--------|---|--------|
| green  | = | greet  |
| yellow | = | mellow |

| corn    | = | torn    |
|---------|---|---------|
| peas    | = | pets    |
| pumpkin | = | bumpkin |

| couch | = | touch |
|-------|---|-------|
| chair | = | choir |
| table | = | sable |

1. _____
2. _____
3. _____
4. _____
5. _____
6. _____
7. _____
8. _____
9. _____
10. _____

# Numbers and General Information

Each number represents a common standard or value connected with general information.

> **Example:** 26 L of the A = 26 letters of the alphabet

1. 7 D of the W  _____
2. 52 C in a D  _____
3. 12 M in a Y  _____
4. 50 S in the U S  _____
5. 60 M in an H  _____
6. 18 H on a G C  _____
7. 4 Q in a D  _____
8. 3 S on a T  _____
9. 52 W in a Y  _____
10. 9 P on a B T  _____
11. 24 H in a D  _____
12. 36 I in a Y  _____
13. 100 Y in a C  _____
14. 2 P in a Q  _____
15. 365 D in a Y  _____

# Double Meaning Deduction

Write the words that are being defined. All of the answers will relate to a common theme. Write the theme on the line.

a. to go faster than a walk  _____

b. "home" to military personnel  _____

c. knocking all 10 pins down in bowling  _____

d. a common stone for an engagement ring  _____

e. container for lemonade  _____

f. a mitten with fingers  _____

g. what Cinderella went to  _____

h. opposite of *in*  _____

What is being described? _____

♦ ♦ ♦ ♦ ♦ ♦ ♦ ♦ ♦ ♦ ♦ ♦ ♦ ♦ ♦ ♦ ♦ ♦ ♦ ♦

a. an elephant's nose  _____

b. to grow weary  _____

c. the top of one's mouth  _____

d. islands in Florida  _____

e. the car that pulls a train  _____

f. comes before the Queen in a deck of cards  _____

g. the part of a jacket or poncho that covers your head  _____

h. a spectator at a baseball game  _____

What is being described? _____

# Double Meaning Deduction

Write the words that are being defined. All of the answers will relate to a common theme. Write the theme on the line.

a. black parts of the eyes _____

b. enclosures for pigs _____

c. having style or sophistication _____

d. another name for kings or monarchs _____

e. what a doctor does to check you over _____

f. people who participate in an experiment _____

g. Someone who lives in Great Britian is this nationality. _____

h. what a pedigree dog has _____

Where am I? _____

◆ ◆ ◆ ◆ ◆ ◆ ◆ ◆ ◆ ◆ ◆ ◆ ◆ ◆ ◆ ◆ ◆ ◆ ◆ ◆

a. a section of a building _____

b. a common household insect _____

c. what police give for speeding _____

d. to stumble over something _____

e. flying by the _____ of your pants _____

f. to broadcast on television _____

g. the light on a gas range _____

h. You buy an acre of this to plant crops. _____

What is it? _____

# Deduction Puzzles

Using the clues, determine which teacher is in each room and which subject is being taught.

|  | Room 222 | Room 223 | Room 224 | Room 225 | Room 226 |
|---|---|---|---|---|---|
| Teacher |  |  |  |  |  |
| Subject |  |  |  |  |  |

1. The math teacher's room is at the beginning of the hall.
2. Mr. Miller is a history teacher.
3. Miss Lee teaches in room 223.
4. Latin is taught in room 226.
5. Mrs. Burns and Miss Lee's rooms are next to each other.
6. The computer instructor is in room 223.
7. The art teacher's room is next to the Latin teacher's room.
8. Room 224 is occupied by the history teacher.
9. The Latin teacher is Mrs. Smith.
10. Ms. Johns is a good friend of Mrs. Burns.

Using the clues, determine the names of each person's mother and father.

|  | Sally | Joe | Mary | Tom | Sarah |
|---|---|---|---|---|---|
| Mother |  |  |  |  |  |
| Father |  |  |  |  |  |

1. Mary's mother is Paula.
2. Bev has a daughter.
3. Sam and Maria are married.
4. Sally's mother is Jane.
5. Gus is Sarah's father.
6. Mary's father is not Dick.
7. Paula is married to Pete.
8. Tom's father is Chuck.
9. Theresa is not Joe's mother.

# Deduction Puzzles

Using the clues, determine who owns each store and what type of stores are in the mall.

|  | Store 1 | Store 2 | Store 3 | Store 4 | Store 5 |
|---|---|---|---|---|---|
| Owner |  |  |  |  |  |
| Type |  |  |  |  |  |

1. The drugstore owner is next to Leroy's store.
2. Phil owns the second store.
3. Leroy runs the middle store.
4. The grocery store is nearest to the main entrance.
5. The card shop is owned by Alice.
6. Henrí owns the last store.
7. Mac owns a store on one of the ends.
8. The barbershop is not on an end.
9. Henrí owns the pet store.

Using the clues, determine who owns which pet and where each one lives.

|  | dog | horse | cat | fish |
|---|---|---|---|---|
| Owner |  |  |  |  |
| Home |  |  |  |  |

1. There is a dog on the ranch.
2. Someone lives on a farm.
3. Jane does not live on the farm.
4. Dave owns the horse.
5. Carmen owns a cat.
6. The town house is owned by Tomas.
7. The horse is not owned by the apartment dweller.

## Deduction Puzzles

Using the clues, determine who drives which type of vehicle and in which city each person works.

|  | Rick | Pete | Sam | José | Ralph |
|---|---|---|---|---|---|
| Vehicle |  |  |  |  |  |
| City |  |  |  |  |  |

1. The New Yorker drives a cab.
2. Sam works in Chicago.
3. José does not work in Philadelphia.
4. Ralph works in San Francisco.
5. Pete engineers a train.
6. José drives a bus.
7. The airplane pilot does not work in Philadelphia.
8. The trolley driver works in San Francisco.
9. Someone works in Las Vegas.

Using the clues, determine who drove which car and what place each driver took in the race.

|  | Lane 1 | Lane 2 | Lane 3 | Lane 4 |
|---|---|---|---|---|
| Driver |  |  |  |  |
| Car |  |  |  |  |
| Place |  |  |  |  |

1. Willie won the race.
2. The Mustang was not in Lane 2.
3. Drag took second place.
4. B.J. drove a Camaro.
5. The Trans Am placed second.
6. The Toyota ran in Lane 4.
7. Race drove in Lane 3.
8. The car in Lane 1 took third place.
9. The Mustang came in fourth.

# Deduction Puzzles

Using the clues, determine how many years each man served, in which country each was stationed, and during which war each served.

|  | General | Major | Captain | Sergeant | Corporal |
|---|---|---|---|---|---|
| Years served |  |  |  |  |  |
| Country |  |  |  |  |  |
| War |  |  |  |  |  |

1. The captain served in North Korea.
2. The corporal served for one year.
3. The soldier in North Korea served for four years.
4. The sergeant served in England during World War I.
5. The soldier who fought in the Korean War served for four years.
6. The Vietnam War veteran was stationed in Laos.
7. The man who served for five years was stationed in France.
8. The General and the Major served in World War II.
9. The soldier who was stationed in the United States served for fifteen years.
10. The Major served for five years.
11. The soldier in England served three years.

Using the clues, determine who gives which kind of flower to his wife and in which month.

|  | Banker | Lawyer | Doctor | Singer |
|---|---|---|---|---|
| Flower |  |  |  |  |
| Month |  |  |  |  |

1. The singer gives his wife carnations.
2. Someone gives roses, but it is not the banker.
3. In April, this man's wife receives lilies.
4. The lawyer gives his wife flowers in September.
5. One wife receives roses in October.
6. Daffodils are given by someone other than the doctor.
7. Someone gives flowers in June, but it is not the banker.

## Deduction Puzzles

Using the clues, determine which country each missionary is in, what his religion is, and how many years of service he has provided.

|  | Stan | Larry | Clyde | Charles | Art |
|---|---|---|---|---|---|
| Years served |  |  |  |  |  |
| Religion |  |  |  |  |  |
| Country |  |  |  |  |  |

1. The Mormon has been a missionary for 12 years.
2. Larry is not the Catholic.
3. One missionary has been in Ireland for 7 years.
4. The Belgium missionary has served for 9 years.
5. The Methodist has been a missionary for 7 years.
6. The Presbyterian has been in the mission field for 4 years.
7. Art serves in Belgium.
8. Charles has served for 12 years, but not in Africa.
9. The Lutheran missionary works in Switzerland.
10. One missionary has been in the field for 3 years.
11. Stan is Presbyterian.
12. Clyde is a missionary in Switzerland.
13. One missionary has been in Denmark for 12 years.

Using the clues, determine who hosts which game show.

|  | Channel 2 | Channel 5 | Channel 7 | Channel 9 | Channel 11 |
|---|---|---|---|---|---|
| Show |  |  |  |  |  |
| Host |  |  |  |  |  |

1. Burt does not host "Guess My Job."
2. Bob hosts the game show "Rummy."
3. "Win a Trip" is hosted by Billy.
4. "Deal 'Em" is shown on Channel 11.
5. "Win a Trip" is not shown on Channel 2.
6. "Rummy" is the show on Channel 5.
7. "Clues" is aired on Channel 7.
8. Barney works for Channel 2.
9. Buzz works for Channel 11.

# Deduction Puzzles

Using the clues, determine the name and breed of each person's dog.

|  | Diane | Nancy | Marla | Kathy | Ann |
|---|---|---|---|---|---|
| Name |  |  |  |  |  |
| Breed |  |  |  |  |  |

1. Fido is a mixed breed.
2. The terrier belongs to Diane.
3. Cinnamon is a chow chow.
4. Nancy does not own Rex.
5. Ann owns a German shepherd.
6. Kathy does not own the poodle or the mixed breed.
7. Marla owns Fifi.
8. Skippy is a terrier.

Using the clues, determine which college each woman attends, what year she is in, and which gymnastic event is her specialty.

|  | Mary | Megan | Maxine | Molly |
|---|---|---|---|---|
| Year of College |  |  |  |  |
| Event |  |  |  |  |
| College |  |  |  |  |

1. The gymnast from Ohio State does not excel in the floor exercises.
2. Megan is a sophomore.
3. The girl in Virginia performs on the uneven parallel bars.
4. Mary goes to Penn State University.
5. Molly goes to the University of Maryland.
6. The freshman goes to the University of Virginia.
7. The junior is best at vaulting.
8. Maxine is best on the uneven parallel bars.
9. Molly is not a senior.
10. The senior does not do a balance beam routine.

# Roman Numeral Conversion

Convert the numbers in the box into Roman numerals. Then complete each word.

> **Example:** 11 = XI = E<u>XI</u>T

|  |  |  |
|---|---|---|
| 2000 | 1001 | 201 |
| 101 | 11 | 6 |
| 151 | 4 | 200 |
| 551 | 9 | 506 |

(1 = I   5 = V   10 = X   50 = L   100 = C   500 = D   1000 = M)

1. _____mate

2. di_____sion

3. m_____er

4. su_____er

5. a_____elerate

6. ta_____ng

7. mi_____ne

8. a_____dent

9. dr_____er

10. i_____ng

11. a_____se

12. o_____ssion

*Verbal Reasoning—Convergent Reasoning*
*WALC 9: Verbal and Visual Reasoning*

**Deduction by Exclusion**

Read each direction and cross off the days on the calendar. You'll be left with one date.

| FEBRUARY | | | | | | |
|---|---|---|---|---|---|---|
| Sun | Mon | Tues | Wed | Thur | Fri | Sat |
| | | | 1 | 2<br>Groundhog Day | 3 | 4 |
| 5 | 6 | 7 | 8 | 9 | 10 | 11 |
| 12 | 13 | 14<br>Valentine's Day | 15 | 16 | 17 | 18 |
| 19 | 20 | 21 | 22 | 23 | 24 | 25 |
| 26 | 27 | 28 | | | | |

1. It's not three days before or three days after Valentine's Day.

2. It's not a date that is a multiple of three.

3. It's not a day of the week that has the letter *O* in it.

4. It's not an odd-numbered day.

5. It's not on a weekday.

6. It's not a date with two digits.

Which date is left? _____

# Deduction by Exclusion

Read each direction and cross off the days on the calendar. You'll be left with one date.

| \ | \ | \ | JANUARY | \ | \ | \ |
|---|---|---|---|---|---|---|
| Sun | Mon | Tues | Wed | Thur | Fri | Sat |
|  |  | 1 | 2 | 3 | 4 | 5 |
| 6 | 7 | 8 | 9 | 10 | 11 | 12 |
| 13 | 14 | 15 | 16 | 17 | 18 | 19 |
| 20 | 21 | 22 | 23 | 24 | 25 | 26 |
| 27 | 28 | 29 | 30 | 31 |  |  |

1. It isn't a date that's a multiple of four.
2. It doesn't fall on a weekday that begins with *TH*.
3. It doesn't fall on a date where the two digits are the same.
4. It's not evenly divisible by five.
5. It's not on the second or fourth Sunday of the month.
6. It isn't a date with one digit.
7. It isn't on the weekend.
8. It's not the second Monday of the month.
9. It isn't two days before the 20th.
10. It's not the fourth Wednesday or the last Tuesday.

Which date is left? _____

## Word Search—Opposites

Find the opposites of the words on the list. They can be vertical, horizontal, or diagonal.

| N | I | G | H | T | E | L | D | I |
|---|---|---|---|---|---|---|---|---|
| A | K | M | R | A | D | U | L | T |
| Z | W | R | O | N | G | G | A | A |
| E | N | E | A | R | N | O | B | M |
| D | E | T | L | I | E | O | U | E |
| I | S | T | Y | A | V | D | Y | R |
| E | O | A | E | P | E | A | C | E |
| O | L | C | S | E | R | A | L | H |
| P | C | S | U | M | M | E | R | T |

| | | |
|---|---|---|
| no | open | always |
| child | work | war |
| sit | gather | here |
| right | winter | far |
| bad | truth | hairy |
| wild | day | sell |

# Logic Questions

Answer each question.

1. A bottle and a jar cost $1.10. The bottle costs $1.00 more than the jar. What does each one cost?  _____

2. From 19, take one and leave 20.
   (Hint: Think Roman numerals.)  _____

3. A frog fell into a 20-foot well. Every day it jumps up 3 feet. At night, it falls back 2 feet. At this rate, how many days will it take him to get out of the well?  _____

4. A young man driving some cows was asked how many cows he had. He replied, "When the cows are in line, there are 2 cows ahead of a cow, 2 cows behind a cow, and 1 cow in the middle." How many cows did he have?  _____

5. During dinner, they ate all but 7 of the 15 hamburgers. How many hamburgers were left?  _____

6. What are six words that can be found in HEREIN without transposing a single letter?

   1. _____  4. _____

   2. _____  5. _____

   3. _____  6. _____

# Logic Questions

Answer each question. Think beyond the obvious.

1. What was the largest ocean before Balboa discovered the Pacific Ocean? _____

2. How many crackers can you eat on an empty stomach? _____

3. Three large, muscular men were walking under a regular-sized umbrella but they didn't get wet. Why didn't they get wet? _____

4. What can a box be filled with so it is lighter than when it is full of air? _____

5. The only barber in town likes brunettes to go into his shop. Last week he said, "The truth is that I'd rather give two brunettes haircuts than to give a haircut to one blonde." What is the reasoning behind this? _____

6. A mother has six children and five potatoes. How can she feed each an equal amount of potatoes? (Do not use fractions.) _____

7. Laura decides to ride her white stallion into the forest. How far into the forest can she go? _____

8. My friend Carolyn, the butcher, wears a size 10 shoe, is 5 feet tall, and wears a size 9 coat. What does she weigh? _____

9. Last night, my aunt Linda was able to turn her bedroom light off and get into bed before the room was dark. The light switch and the bed are 12 feet apart. How did she do this? _____

## Logic Questions

Answer each question. Think beyond the obvious.

1. What occurs once in June and twice in August but never occurs in December? _____

2. What can you always find in the middle of *taxicab*? _____

3. What word ends in *T*, contains *VEN*, and starts with *IN*? _____

4. What word becomes *longer* when the third letter is removed? _____

5. A man has 8 sons and each has 1 sister. In total, how many children does the man have? _____

6. It occurs once in a minute, twice in a week, and once in a year. What is it? _____

7. What is in the middle of a cigar? _____

8. How much do 10 pieces of candy cost if one thousand pieces cost $10? _____

9. If "two's company" and "three's a crowd," what is four and five? _____

10. Among my cohorts, I am the narrowest. I am in Paris but I am not in France. What am I? _____

# Logic Questions

Answer each question. Think beyond the obvious.

1. A doctor has a brother who is an attorney in Chicago, but the attorney in Chicago does not have a brother who is a doctor. How is this possible? _____

2. Pete asks, "If Chuck's son is my son's father, how am I related to Chuck?" _____

3. If your uncle's sister is related to you but she is not your aunt, what is the relation? _____

4. A group of explorers found a cave. One of them is congratulated by a younger son who then sends a telegram to his father telling of the discovery. Who discovered the cave? _____

5. Can a man marry his brother's wife's mother-in-law? _____

6. Is a man allowed to marry his widow's sister? _____

7. Danielle is looking at the portrait of a man. She says, "He's not my father but his mother was my mother's mother-in-law." Who is the man? _____

8. A man was looking at a photograph. He said, "Brothers and sisters? I have none but this man's son is my father's son." Who was in the photograph? _____

9. A woman was looking at a photograph. She said, "Brothers and sisters? I have one. And this man's father is my father's son." Who was in the photograph? _____

# Word Wheel

Create words by moving from one letter to another that's connected. You can use a letter more than once. The letters must be connected on the wheel in the same order as the word you want to build. The words should be three letters or more.

> **Example:** You can build the word *east*, but not the word *seat* because the letter *A* isn't connected to the letter *T*.

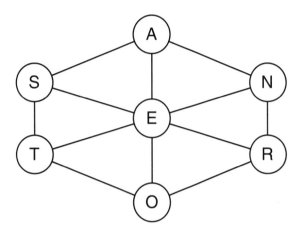

1. _____
2. _____
3. _____
4. _____
5. _____
6. _____
7. _____
8. _____
9. _____
10. _____

11. _____
12. _____
13. _____
14. _____
15. _____
16. _____
17. _____
18. _____
19. _____
20. _____

# Build the Answer

Fill in the answers on the grid using the clues. The letters in the circles will spell out the answer to the question at the bottom of the page.

1. a woman who rules over a kingdom
2. a reptile with a shell
3. breezy
4. the seed on an oak tree
5. where you go out to eat
6. what you take with a camera
7. worn on a scuba diver's feet
8. the ground between mountains
9. a two-wheeled vehicle propelled by pedaling
10. decayed, spoiled, rancid
11. opposite of *same*

What number is written as 1 followed by 18 zeros? _____

# Combined Associated Words

Cross out the letters as described in each item. The letters for each word are in order. Then write both words on the line.

> **Example:** Cross out the bird and leave its home.   ~~r~~n~~o~~e~~b~~s~~i~~t   robin, nest

1. Cross out the animal and leave its home.  ldieonn  _____

2. Cross out the state and leave the city.  IdBoaishoe  _____

3. Cross out the fire and leave what burns.  flpaapmeer  _____

4. Cross out the tree and leave its nut.  oaacorkn  _____

5. Cross out the emotion and leave the facial expression.  hsamppinileess  _____

6. Cross out the sport and leave the equipment.  bgalseobvaell  _____

7. Cross out the event and leave the performer.  ccirlowcuns  _____

8. Cross out the suit and leave the card.  hjeaacrkts  _____

9. Cross out the month and leave the day.  JMuonndaey  _____

10. Cross out the temperature and leave the weather.  cosnlowdy  _____

11. Cross out the ocean and leave the river.  PNaciilfiec  _____

12. Cross out the man and leave his discovery.  Felraecntrkilciinty  _____

13. Cross out the building and leave the room.  hoduesne  _____

14. Cross out the animal and leave its baby.  ckiattten  _____

# Combined Associated Words

Cross out the letters as described in each item. The letters for each word are in order. Then write both words on the line.

> **Example:** Cross out the bird and leave its home.   r̸o̸b̸i̸n̸e̸s̸t̸   robin, nest

1. Cross out the fish and leave the bait.   fwloounrdmer   _____
2. Cross out the food and leave the drink.   sctofefaeke   _____
3. Cross out the meal and leave the dessert.   dicnankere   _____
4. Cross out the stone and leave the metal.   gcroappneirte   _____
5. Cross out the school and leave the subject.   coEnIglliesghe   _____
6. Cross out the furniture and leave the material.   csoauticnh   _____
7. Cross out the container and leave the food.   cacerrteaoln   _____
8. Cross out the sport and leave the equipment.   hpouckckey   _____
9. Cross out the month and leave the day.   ATuuesgudasyt   _____
10. Cross out the tool and leave the hardware.   hnaamilmer   _____
11. Cross out the spice and leave the container.   sshaakletr   _____
12. Cross out the clothing and leave the fastener.   jzaipckpeert   _____
13. Cross out the jewelry and leave the gemstone.   beramceerleatld   _____
14. Cross out the building and leave the cash.   bmoanneyk   _____

# Separating

Separate the combined words in each item. The letters for each word are in order. A clue is given for each set of words.

▶ **Example:** two animals     cdaotg    <u>cat</u>    <u>dog</u>

1. two things you read    bmaogazoinke    _____ _____
2. two colors    pgurrpeelne    _____ _____
3. two animals    tibgeearr    _____ _____
4. two pieces of furniture    ctahbalire    _____ _____
5. two articles of clothing    sphianrtts    _____ _____
6. two body parts    leelbogw    _____ _____
7. two numbers    tseevnen    _____ _____
8. two wall hangings    pmicitrureror    _____ _____
9. two occupations    cbharebfer    _____ _____
10. two trees    msapplruece    _____ _____
11. two sports    bgaoselbfall    _____ _____
12. two birds    rworbenin    _____ _____
13. two emotions    haanppgeinress    _____ _____
14. two desserts    cpiakee    _____ _____
15. two spices    pceinpnapmeron    _____ _____

# Separating

Separate the combined words in each item. The letters for each word are in order. A clue is given for each set of words.

▶ **Example:** two animals     cdaotg    <u>cat</u>    <u>dog</u>

1. two types of music     jroaczzk    _____ _____

2. two colors     oyraenglleow    _____ _____

3. two sports     btorxiangck    _____ _____

4. two things you wear on your feet     sslhipoepesrs    _____ _____

5. two rooms in a house     bkeitdcrohoemn    _____ _____

6. two articles of clothing     blcoouaset    _____ _____

7. two writing implements     pceranyocinl    _____ _____

8. two sharp items     kscinissfoers    _____ _____

9. two kinds of water transportation     scahniope    _____ _____

10. two kinds of fish     fltouunndear    _____ _____

11. two window coverings     sblhiadndess    _____ _____

12. two of your senses     ssigmehltl    _____ _____

13. two insects     waanstp    _____ _____

14. two pieces of silverware     fknorifke    _____ _____

15. two things you mail     plosettctaerdr    _____ _____

## Numerical Sequences

Complete each number sequence.

1. 1, 2, 3, 4, 5, ____, ____, ____

2. 1, 2, ____, ____, 5, 6, ____, ____, 9, ____

3. 2, 4, 6, ____, ____, ____, 14

4. 1, 3, 5, ____, ____, ____, ____

5. 15, 14, 13, ____, ____, ____, 9, 8

6. 20, 18, 16, ____, ____, ____, 8, 6

7. 5, 10, 15, ____, ____, 30, 35

8. 100, 95, 90, 85, ____, ____, ____, 65

9. 10, 20, 30, ____, ____, 60, 70

10. 90, 80, ____, ____, 50, 40

11. 3, 6, 9, 12, ____, ____, 21

12. 30, 27, 24, ____, ____, 15, 12

13. 1, 8, ____, 22, 29

14. 100, 94, 88, ____, ____, 70

15. 8, 12, ____, ____, ____, 28

16. 40, 36, ____, 28, ____, ____, 16

17. 15, 30, ____, 60, ____

18. 0, 8, 16, ____, ____, 40, 48

19. 13, 26, 52, ____, ____, 416

20. 600, 300, 150, ____

## Numerical Sequences

Complete each number sequence. Hint: These have two-step sequences.

1. 10, 20, 17, 34, 31, ____, ____

2. 5, 10, 11, 22, 23, ____, ____

3. 200, 100, 104, 52, 56, ____, ____

4. 2, 12, 10, 20, 18, ____, ____

5. 5, 15, 20, 60, 65, ____, ____

6. 10, 6, 14, 10, 18, ____, ____

7. 600, 300, 320, 160, 180, ____, ____

8. 2718, 906, 900, 300, 294, ____, ____

9. 2, 7, 14, 19, 38, ____, ____

10. 57, 54, 52, 49, 47, ____, ____

11. 4, 16, 8, 32, 16, ____, ____

12. 12, 7, 21, 16, 48, ____, ____

13. 1000, 500, 496, 248, 244, ____, ____

14. 16, 28, 32, 44, 48, ____, ____

15. 15, 18, 36, 39, 78, ____, ____

16. 5, 25, 24, 120, 119, ____, ____

17. 5, 3, 8, 6, 11, ____, ____

18. 10, 16, 48, 54, 162, ____, ____

19. 25, 20, 60, 55, 165, ____, ____

20. 4, 14, 28, 38, 76, ____, ____

## Acrostics

Use the clues to determine the saying in the puzzle. The numbers of the letters correspond to the numbers in the puzzle.

A. proof that can be used in a trial  __45__ __12__ __3__ __37__ __29__ __49__ __17__ __8__

B. what a king sits on  __22__ __47__ __34__ __24__ __16__ __11__

C. a housekeeper  __25__ __31__ __48__ __14__

D. a long time period  __36__ __41__ __28__

E. the opposite of *gives*  __5__ __21__ __7__ __15__ __42__

F. trenches around a castle  __2__ __43__ __1__ __33__ __23__

G. a kind of carpet  __32__ __20__ __6__ __50__

H. one of the things in your mouth  __46__ __27__ __39__ __19__ __30__

I. neckwear for men  __38__ __35__ __26__ __10__

J. singular of the verb *to be*  __9__ __4__

K. a coin worth 10 cents  __40__ __13__ __44__ __18__

## Acrostics

Use the clues to determine the saying in the puzzle. The numbers of the letters correspond to the numbers in the puzzle.

A. between sunset and sunrise  __ __ __ __ __
                                4  17  14  34  28

B. equals 60 seconds  __ __ __ __ __ __
                      2  3  33  36  22  27

C. what you walk on  __ __ __ __ __
                     9  42  12  38  26

D. what many people live in  __ __ __ __ __
                             29  25  13  18  7

E. not this one, but _____ one  __ __ __ __
                                 16  15  1  6

F. opposite of *man*  __ __ __ __ __
                     19  8  24  32  31

G. an eating utensil  __ __ __ __
                      39  20  37  43

H. to harm or cause pain  __ __ __ __
                          23  5  21  40

I. a grain  __ __ __
            35  41  10

J. a sound of laughter  __ __
                        11  30

## Describe Without Naming

Describe these items/terms without using their names.

1. grandfather's clock
2. softness
3. carpet
4. trust
5. pirate
6. heart
7. running
8. democracy
9. ship
10. story
11. yogurt
12. emergency
13. bells
14. computer
15. coast
16. vest
17. natural
18. alarm
19. nation
20. fast-food restaurant
21. worm
22. aluminum can
23. nail file
24. paint
25. fishing pole
26. cheese
27. seat belt
28. octopus
29. bridge
30. apartment
31. electric can opener
32. sailboat
33. trophy
34. hamburger
35. snow
36. rock
37. trial
38. water
39. August
40. odometer

## Advertisements

Give a one- or two-minute advertisement for each product.

1. a remote-control lawn mower
2. a plant that never needs watering
3. a car that gets 175 miles per gallon of gas
4. an eternal youth pill
5. a voice-run computer
6. a dust-free house
7. a pair of shoes that have springs built into the soles
8. a pen that never runs out of ink
9. a sailboat that will never tip over
10. a voice-activated television
11. grass that never needs to be mowed
12. unbreakable windows
13. clothing that makes you invisible
14. a picture telephone
15. low-calorie candy
16. pets that talk
17. an electric fishing hook
18. clothing that never needs to be washed
19. a food that makes you a genius
20. chewing gum that never loses its taste

# Analogies

We think analogously throughout the day. When we make comparisons between people, we use analogous relationships (e.g., Mary has blonde hair, Susan is a redhead). When we are trying to decide what to eat for lunch, we may process "If I am really hungry, I will get a hamburger but if I am not very hungry, I will just get a salad." If we are trying to decide what breed of puppy to buy, we may think "the Labrador is friendly but the poodle is more reserved." This form of reasoning helps in our ability to compare and contrast items and to make fact-based decisions based on the relationships.

Analogies incorporate multiple levels of verbal reasoning. They require your client to determine the relationship between the first set of items. To do so, your client must use the following processes:

- opposites
- part/whole
- synonyms
- characteristics
- word meaning
- associated words
- object/function
- object/place
- location
- categorization
- numerical reasoning

Once your client has determined the relationship, he needs to retain the process and apply it to the second set of items in the analogy. This is a difficult task as frequently your client will try to solve the analogy as two separate entities. Thus, the format of the tasks in this section approach solving analogies from various directions to stimulate flexibility and insure that the process is truly understood and applied to both sets of the analogy.

## Completing Analogies

Fill in the missing part of each analogy.

1. Happy is to glad as sad is to _____.

2. Doctor is to medicine as banker is to _____.

3. Beans are to chili as eggs are to _____.

4. Steering wheel is to car as handlebars are to _____.

5. Chicken is to poultry as mouse is to _____.

6. Three is to triangle as four is to _____.

7. Red is to stop as yellow is to _____.

8. Acrophobia is to heights as claustrophobia is to _____.

9. Cleopatra is to Antony as Juliet is to _____.

10. Mother is to child as lioness is to _____.

11. Grass is to yard as cement is to _____.

12. Zipper is to pants as buttons are to _____.

13. Charlie Brown is to *Peanuts* as Dorothy is to _____.

14. Sunrise is to east as sunset is to _____.

15. Heart is to pump blood as stomach is to _____.

16. Book is to read as aspirin is to _____.

17. Cheer is to stadium as whisper is to _____.

18. Cucumbers are to pickles as cabbage is to _____.

19. Cactus is to desert as seaweed is to _____.

20. Paint is to wall as varnish is to _____.

# Analogies—Complete the Second Half

Fill in the missing parts of the analogy.

1. Hair is to head as _____ is to _____.
2. Grand Canyon is to Arizona as _____ is to _____.
3. Blue is to sky as _____ is to _____.
4. Den is to lion as _____ is to _____.
5. Ink is to pen as _____ is to _____.
6. White is to snow as _____ is to _____.
7. Refrigerator is to electricity as _____ is to _____.
8. Television is to watch as _____ is to _____.
9. Sante Fe is to New Mexico as _____ is to _____.
10. Doctor is to hospital as _____ is to _____.
11. Rug is to floor as _____ is to _____.
12. Hot is to fire as _____ is to _____.
13. Cantaloupe is to fruit as _____ is to _____.
14. Fingers are to hand as _____ are to _____.
15. Plane is to sky as _____ is to _____.
16. Six is to four as _____ is to _____.
17. Flower is to rose as _____ is to _____.
18. Tie is to man as _____ is to _____.
19. Glove is to baseball as _____ is to _____.
20. Swim is to fish as _____ is to _____.

# Analogies—Complete the Second Half

Fill in the missing parts of the analogy.

1. Whale is to mammal as _____ is to _____.
2. Notes are to music as _____ are to _____.
3. Water is to ocean as _____ is to _____.
4. Blood is to red as _____ is to _____.
5. Keys are to piano as _____ are to _____.
6. Arrow is to bow as _____ is to _____.
7. Wet is to water as _____ is to _____.
8. Pyramid is to Egypt as _____ is to _____.
9. Army is to land as _____ is to _____.
10. *New York Times* is to newspaper as _____ is to _____.
11. Flounder is to fish as _____ is to _____.
12. Water is to drink as _____ is to _____.
13. Tires are to car as _____ are to _____.
14. Cat is to feline as _____ is to _____.
15. Paddle is to canoe as _____ is to _____.
16. Perfume is to woman as _____ is to _____.
17. Baby is to infant as _____ is to _____.
18. Hot is to coffee as _____ is to _____.
19. Hands are to clock as _____ are to _____.
20. Beef is to meat as _____ is to _____.

# Analogies—Complete the Second Half

Fill in the missing parts of the analogy.

1. Children are to toys as _____ are to _____.
2. Dark is to night as _____ is to _____.
3. Letter is to envelope as _____ is to _____.
4. Frog is to pond as _____ is to _____.
5. Shampoo is to hair as _____ is to _____.
6. Horn is to car as _____ is to _____.
7. Baseball is to throw as _____ is to _____.
8. Chair is to sit as _____ is to _____.
9. Sand is to beach as _____ is to _____.
10. Bird is to chirp as _____ is to _____.
11. London is to England as _____ is to _____.
12. Smile is to happy as _____ is to _____.
13. Warm is to summer as _____ is to _____.
14. Knee is to leg as _____ is to _____.
15. Collar is to shirt as _____ is to _____.
16. Producer is to movie as _____ is to _____.
17. Sofa is to living room as _____ is to _____.
18. Mug is to coffee as _____ is to _____.
19. Necklace is to neck as _____ is to _____.
20. Leaf is to tree as _____ is to _____.

# Analogies—Complete the First Section

Fill in the missing parts of the analogy.

1. _____ is to actor as _____ is to politician.
2. _____ is to see as _____ is to hear.
3. _____ are to foot as _____ are to hand.
4. _____ is to food as _____ is to drink.
5. _____ is to TV as _____ is to radio.
6. _____ is to wood as _____ is to metal.
7. _____ is to doctor as _____ are to dentist.
8. _____ is to down as _____ is to right.
9. _____ is to car as _____ is to airplane.
10. _____ is to dollar bill as _____ is to quarter.
11. _____ is to Valentine's Day as _____ is to Thanksgiving.
12. _____ is to paper as _____ is to glass.
13. _____ is to white as _____ is to red.
14. _____ is to beef as _____ is to pork.
15. _____ is to bird as _____ is to fish.
16. _____ is to the White House as _____ is to the Vatican.
17. _____ is to computer as _____ is to television.
18. _____ is to sour as _____ is to sweet.
19. _____ is to clock as _____ is to calendar.
20. _____ is to morning as _____ is to evening.

# Analogies—Complete the First Section

Fill in the missing parts of the analogy.

1. _____ is to mammal as _____ is to furniture.
2. _____ is to dictionary as _____ is to phone book.
3. _____ is to number as _____ is to letter.
4. _____ is to England as _____ is to France.
5. _____ is to song as _____ is to book.
6. _____ is to black as _____ is to white.
7. _____ is to shirt as _____ is to pants.
8. _____ is to heavy as _____ is to light.
9. _____ is to Italian as _____ is to Chinese.
10. _____ is to bicycle as _____ is to car.
11. _____ is to breakfast as _____ is to lunch.
12. _____ is to Denver as _____ is to San Diego.
13. _____ is to laugh as _____ is to cry.
14. _____ is to thousand as _____ is to hundred.
15. _____ is to zoologist as _____ is to meteorologist.
16. _____ is to east as _____ is to south.
17. _____ is to insect as _____ is to bird.
18. _____ is to swimmer as _____ is to hiker.
19. _____ is to wedding as _____ is to funeral.
20. _____ is to baseball as _____ is to football.

# Paragraph Comprehension

The paragraphs in this section not only involve understanding and recalling content but the questions involve making inferences or reading between the lines. This ability to make inferences is a necessary component in effective verbal reasoning. Your client cannot make accurate determinations if he cannot identify, interpret, and apply the inferential information. This is a skill needed in daily life. For example, when medication specifies *Take on an empty stomach*, you need to make the inference that the pill should be taken before a meal. If the label on a shirt says to wash in cold water only, the inference needs to be made that the shirt is not to be washed in warm water. If an employer says that he wants a worker to make better use of his time, the worker needs to take the appropriate steps to improve his time management skills.

**Story Inferences**

Read each paragraph. Then answer the questions.

> The police officer was apprehensive about entering the abandoned apartment building. She wasn't sure if the electricity was working and it was dark outside. She knew there were at least two gunmen inside. She decided to wait to go inside until backup officers arrived.

1. Why is the police officer apprehensive about entering the building?
2. How can the police officer tell the building is abandoned?
3. Why does the police officer wonder if the electricity is on?
4. What time of day is it?
5. How did the police officer know there were gunmen in the building?
6. Why did the police officer decide to wait for the backup officers?

> She went to the supermarket on the way home from work. It took her several minutes to find an empty parking space. Once inside, she walked through the aisles trying to decide what to have for dinner. She knew her husband would like to cook fish, but her children would rather eat tacos. She decided to get chicken instead, which is her favorite.

1. Where does this story take place?
2. About what time do you think it is?
3. Why do you think the supermarket is so crowded this time of day?
4. How did she get to the supermarket? How do you know?
5. What decision is the woman trying to make?
6. Does the woman have more than one child? How do you know?

## Story Inferences

Read each paragraph. Then answer the questions.

> Nine students from the Hiking Club decided to take a hike through the state park. When they started out, the sun was directly overhead. After hiking several hours, they were tired, hungry, and hot. They began to argue about what they should do next. Half of the group decided to head for home. The remaining students continued to hike directly toward the setting sun.

1. What kind of day do you think it is?
2. At what time did the group start hiking? How do you know?
3. How long did the group hike?
4. Was the group well-prepared for the hike? How do you know?
5. Why did half of the students decide to head for home?
6. In what direction did the ones who turned back hike?

> In the middle of the week, a woman took her car to the car dealer to get a tune-up and have her air conditioning repaired. She had to wait several minutes before someone waited on her. When the mechanic finally appeared, he apologized for the wait. He explained that many of the workers were on their lunch break. She told the mechanic what she wanted done and gave him the keys. The mechanic said her car would be ready the next morning.

1. About what hour of the day is it?
2. What day of the week would you guess it is?
3. What time of year is it? How do you know?
4. What do you think the mechanic was doing before he helped the woman?
5. Why did the woman give the mechanic her keys?
6. What do you think the woman will do if her car isn't ready in the morning?

## Story Inferences

Read each paragraph. Then answer the questions.

> A family entered the animal shelter to choose a puppy. They stood for a long time trying to decide if they wanted the golden retriever or the beagle. The mother asked to see the two puppies. Her child played with each puppy for a few minutes. They decided to buy the beagle because she was the only female and seemed friendlier. They also thought the smaller dog would be better for where they live.

1. Why was it a good idea for the family to choose a puppy from the animal shelter?
2. At least how many people are in this family?
3. Why did the mother want her child to play with each puppy?
4. What differences are there between the two puppies?
5. Why would a friendly dog be important for the family?
6. Where do you think the family lives? How can you tell?

> The couple has been preparing since early this morning. They hope everything will be perfect. The guests are expected to arrive any minute. The couple works together to set the table and to make sure everything is ready. They hear the doorbell ring and people begin coming in. At the end of the evening, everyone thanks the hosts for a wonderful time. Everything turned out great but now the couple is exhausted. They decide to leave the mess and head straight for bed.

1. What is the couple preparing?
2. What might be the special occasion?
3. Is the couple nervous about the event? How do you know?
4. Were a lot of guests at their home? How can you tell?
5. Can you tell if the couple lives in an apartment or a house?
6. What time of day is the party?

# Visual Reasoning

Visual reasoning involves visually perceiving information and interpreting it in the correct manner. When something is perceived incorrectly, problem solving and reasoning skills are affected. The tasks in this section provide a variety of levels of visual stimuli, including pictures, shapes, and figures, to improve your client's ability to see visual stimuli correctly and to correctly interpret it. As your client works through these exercises, he will need to think logically and make judgments about the information he sees. The skills he uses to interpret the visual information will improve his ability to solve problems in his daily life.

# Visual Analogies

The analogies in this section include solving picture analogies and completing figural analogies. Analogies require your client to determine the relationship between the first set of items. Then your client must retain the relationship and apply it to the second set of items in the analogy. This process stimulates thinking logically and linking two sets together.

In the picture analogies, your client will need to determine relationships based on associations, function, object/agent, part/whole, location, and progression. In the figural analogies, your client will need to determine relationships based on size, direction/rotation, shading, part/whole, number of sides or parts, and shape. Effective visual reasoning is contingent upon the ability to identify and utilize these processing patterns.

We utilize the ability to think visually analogously throughout the day. For example, when parking a car, we know that a small car will fit in a small parking spot just as a larger car will fit in a large parking spot or that a large suitcase will fit in a car trunk if it is placed on its side whereas a gym bag will fit upright. Frequently, someone who has brain dysfunction is not able to effectively use this level of visual reasoning in his daily life. The analogies in this section will aid in reestablishing the ability to visually reason which will help determine correct actions in daily activities.

# Picture Analogies

Circle the picture on the right that solves each analogy.

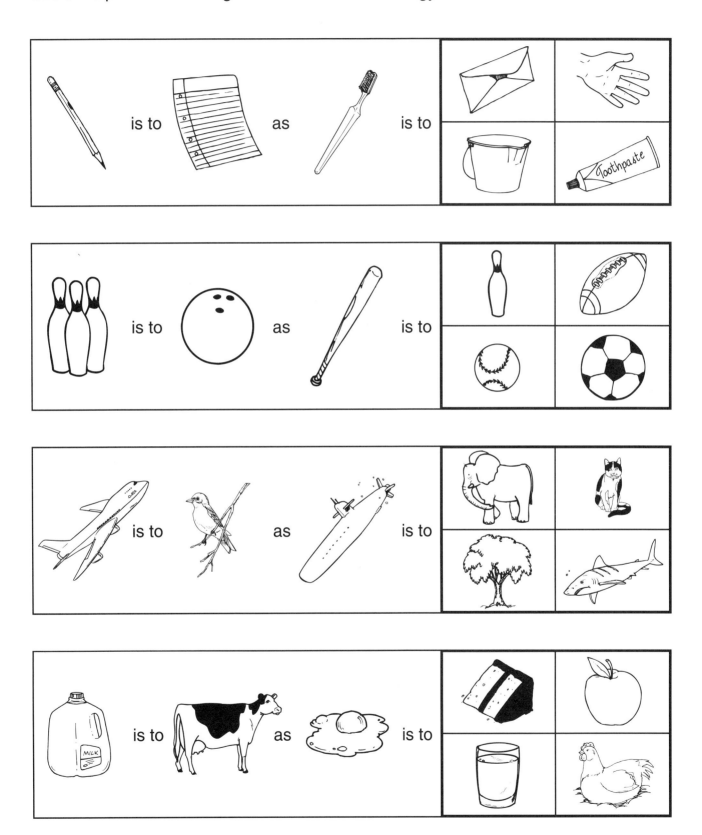

## Picture Analogies

Circle the picture on the right that solves each analogy.

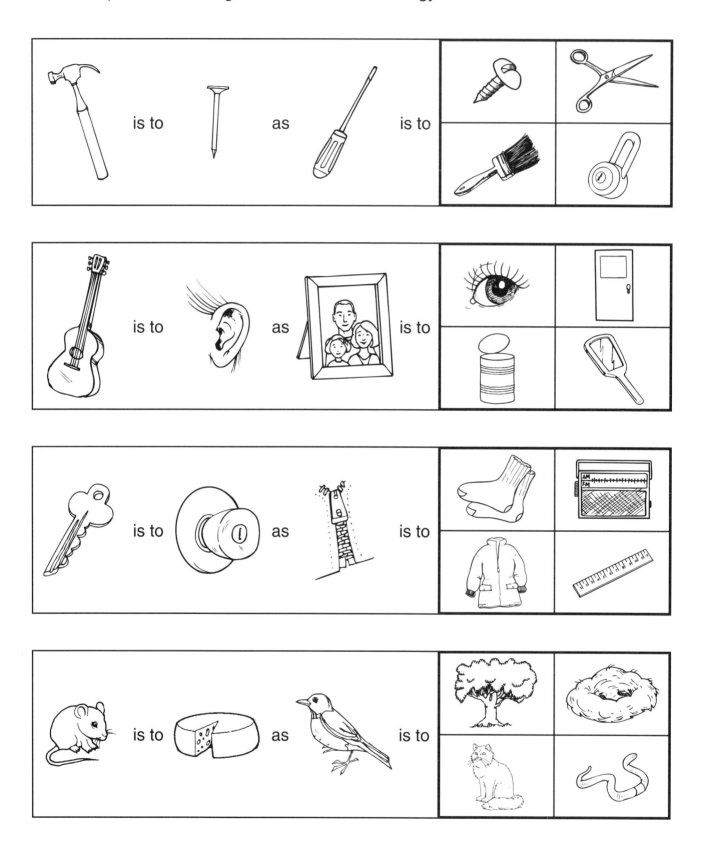

# Picture Analogies

Circle the picture on the right that solves each analogy.

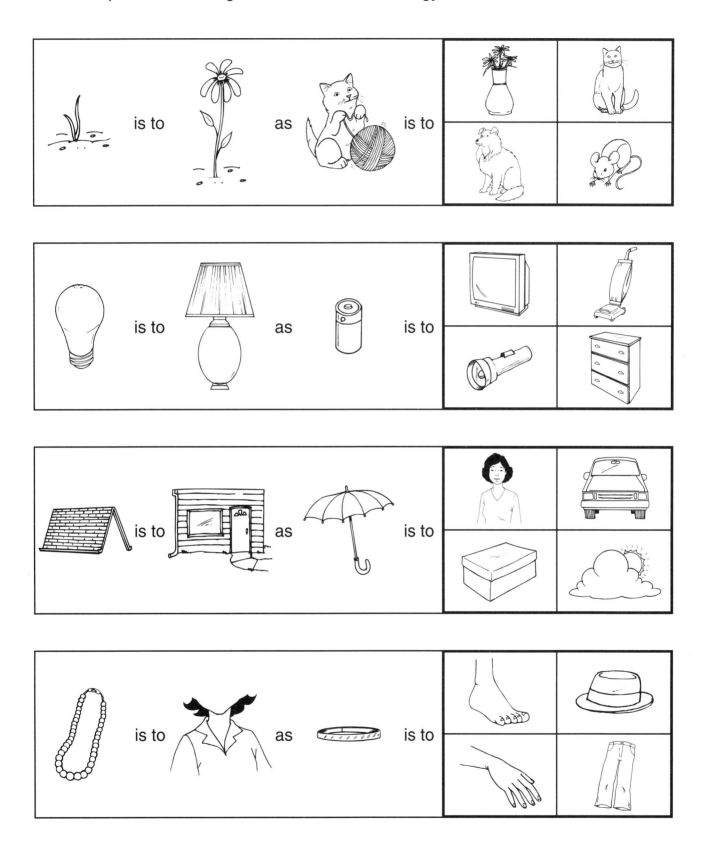

# Picture Analogies

Circle the picture on the right that solves each analogy.

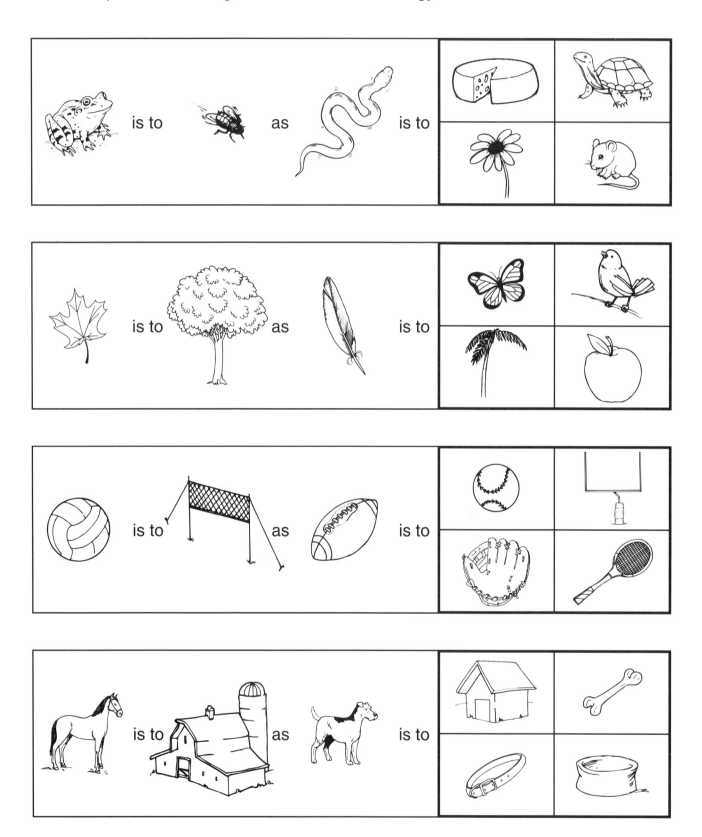

# Figural Analogies—One Factor

Draw the figure to complete each analogy.

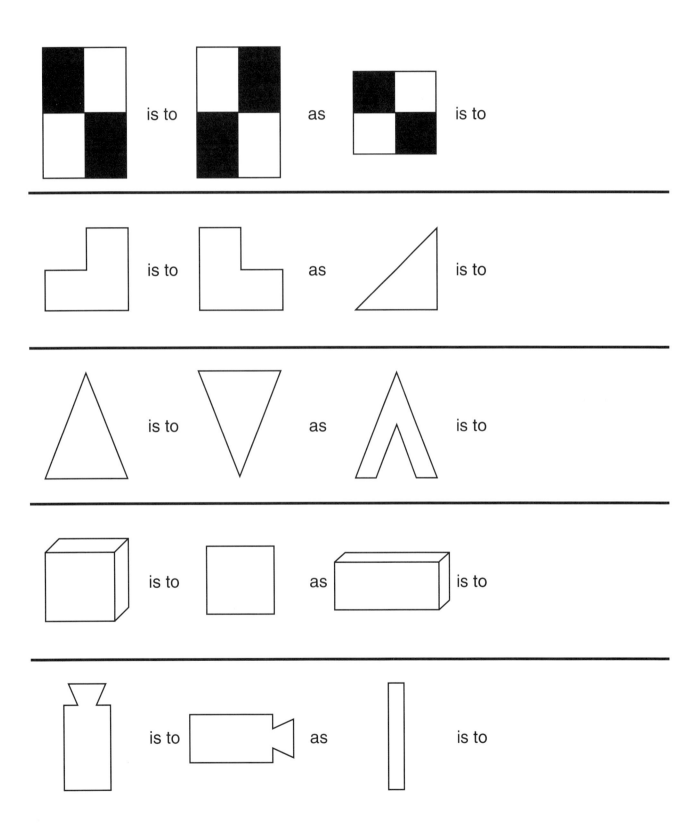

## Figural Analogies—One Factor

Draw the figure to complete each analogy.

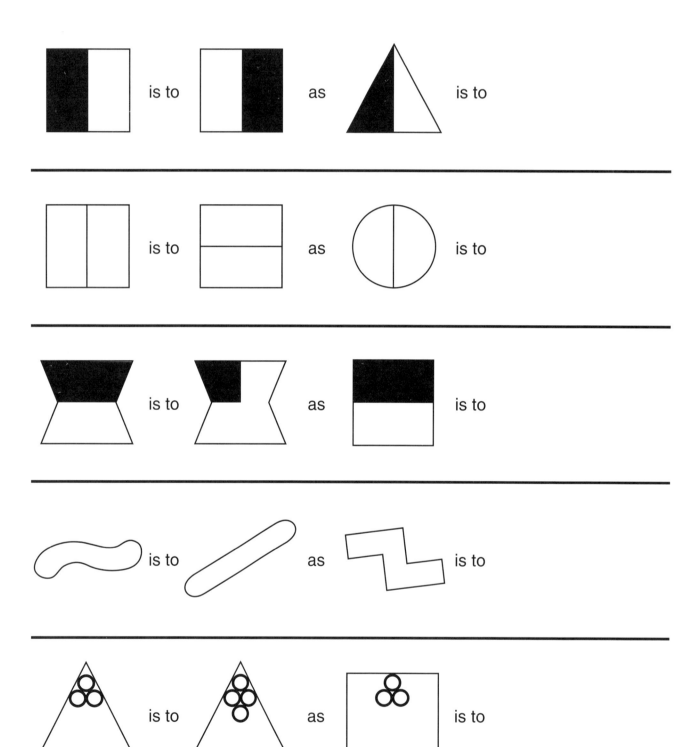

# Figural Analogies—One Factor

Draw the figure to complete each analogy.

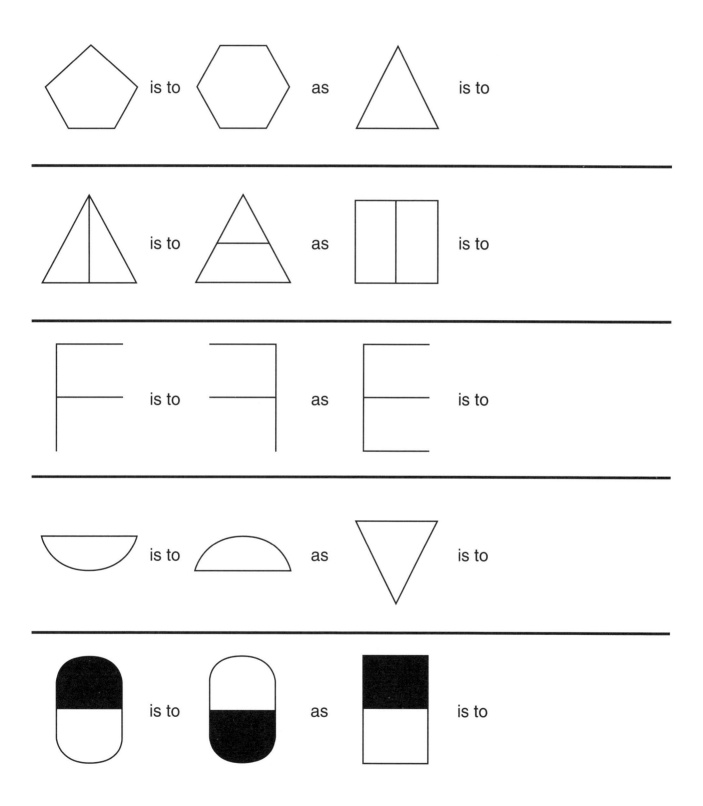

# Figural Analogies—Two Factors

Draw the figure to complete each analogy.

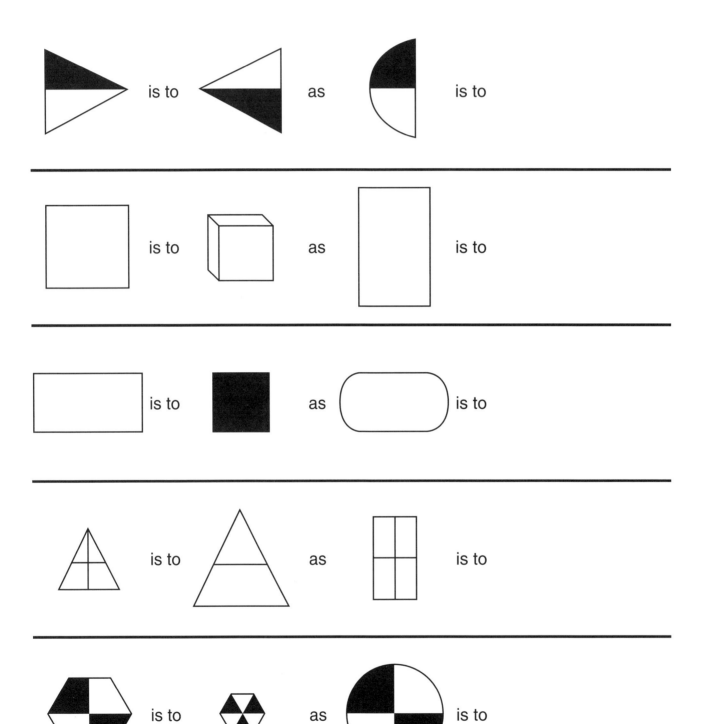

# Figural Analogies—Two Factors

Draw the figure to complete each analogy.

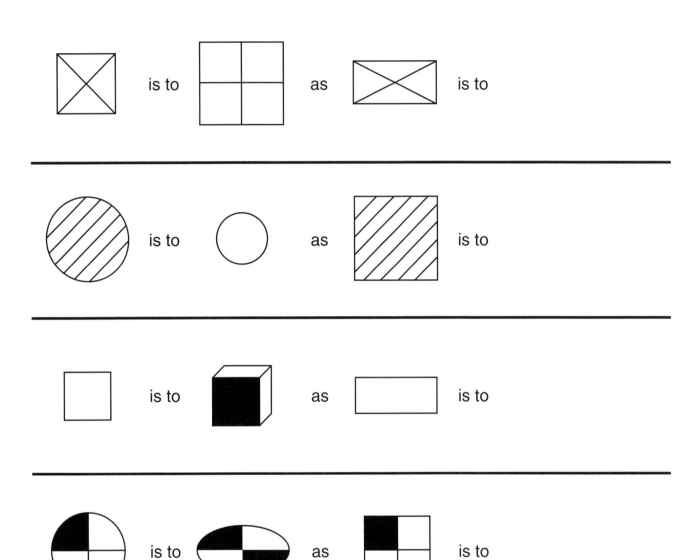

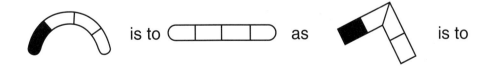

# Figural Analogies—Two Factors

Draw the figure to complete each analogy.

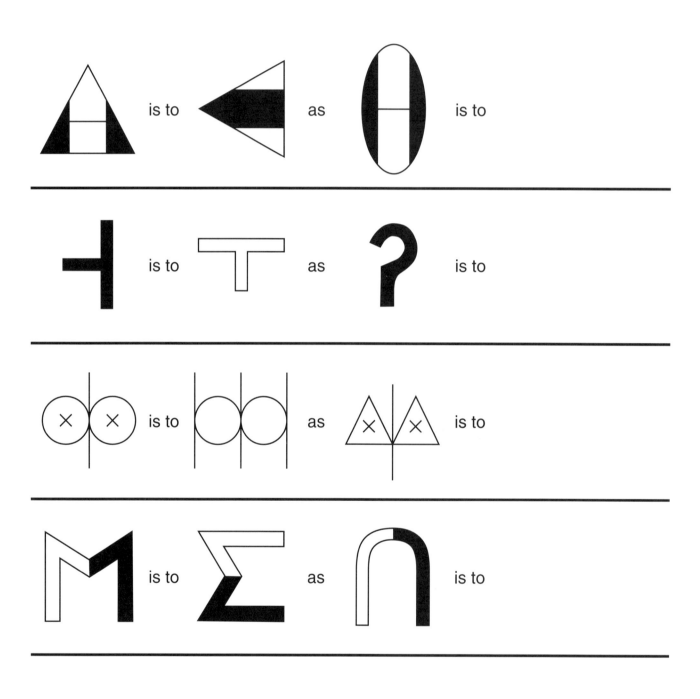

## Figural Analogies—Three Factors

Draw the figure to complete each analogy.

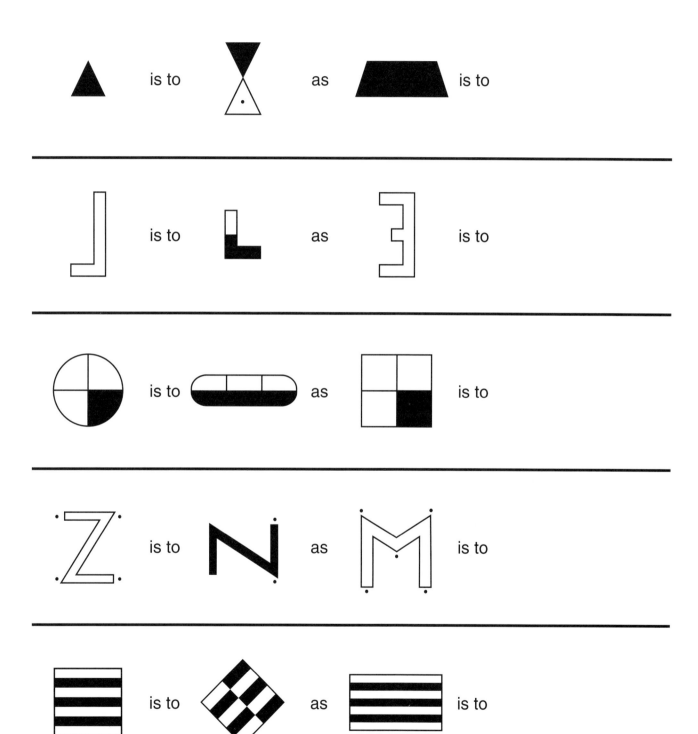

## Figural Analogies—Three Factors

Draw the figure to complete each analogy.

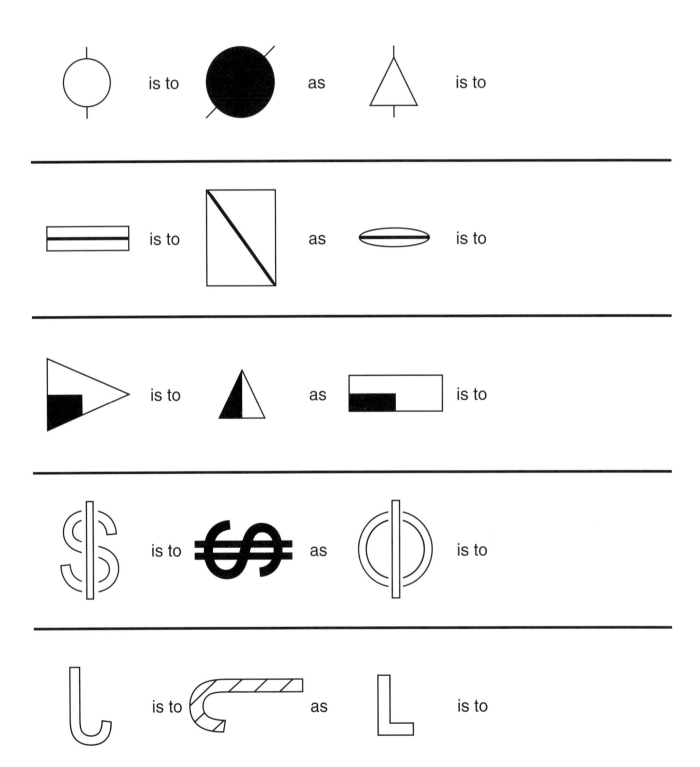

# Figural Analogies—Three Factors

Draw the figure to complete each analogy.

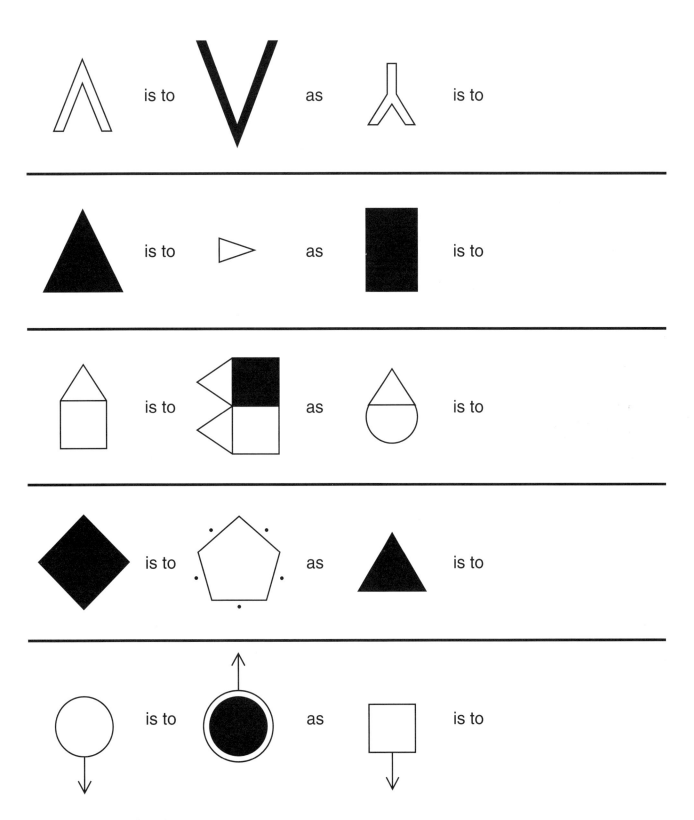

# Drawing Analogy Pairs—One Factor

Look at each analogy pair. Then draw its match to complete each analogy.

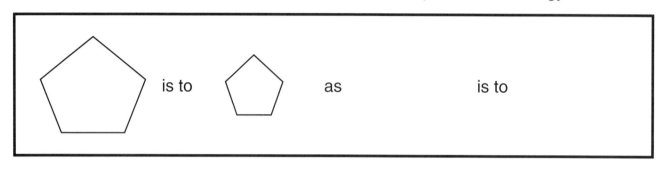

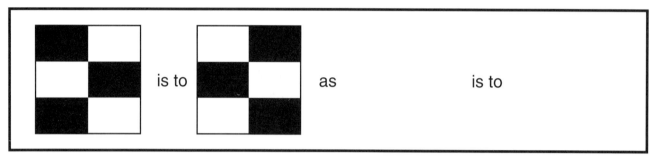

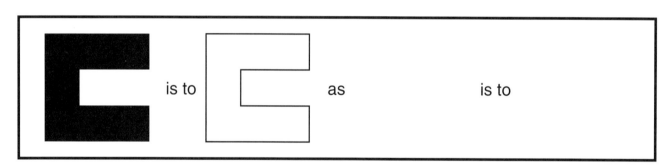

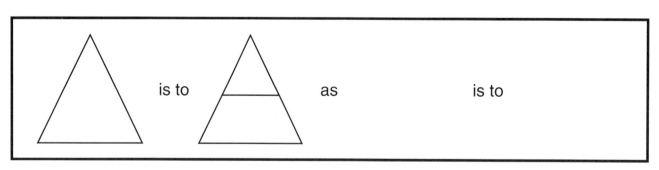

# Drawing Analogy Pairs—One Factor

Look at each analogy pair. Then draw its match to complete each analogy.

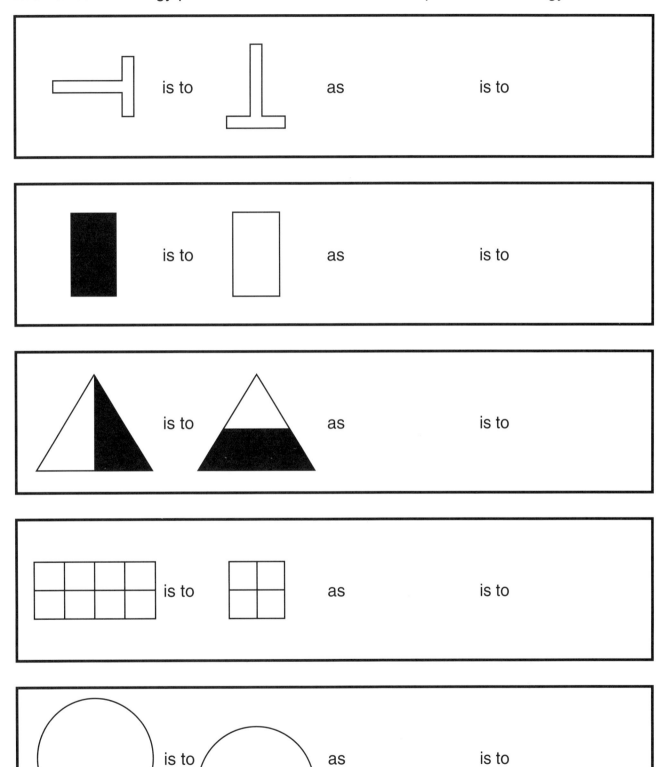

# Drawing Analogy Pairs—Two Factors

Look at each analogy pair. Then draw its match to complete each analogy.

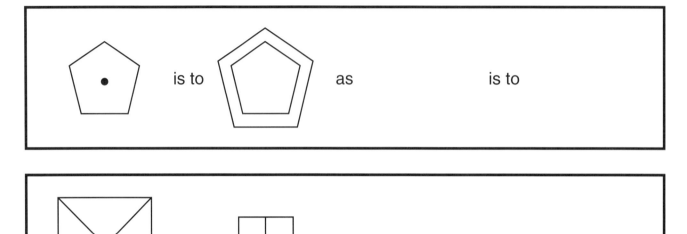

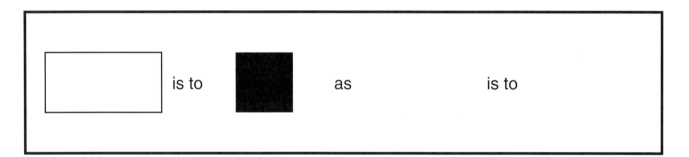

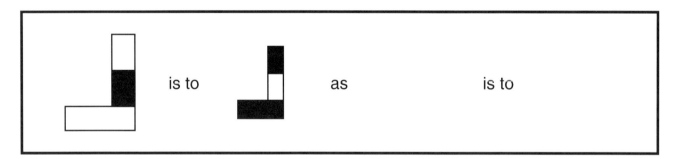

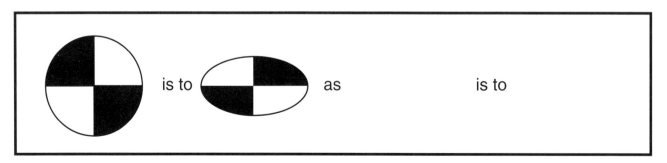

# Drawing Analogy Pairs—Two Factors

Look at each analogy pair. Then draw its match to complete each analogy.

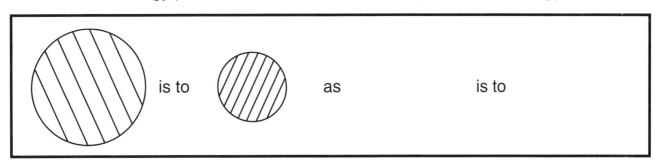

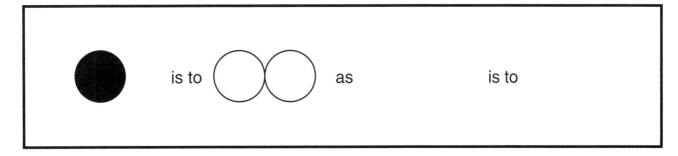

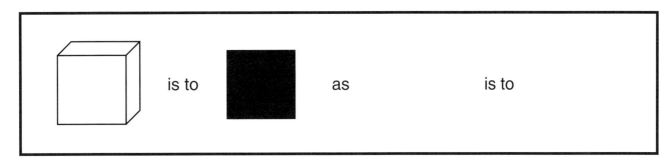

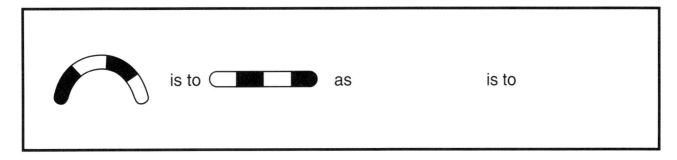

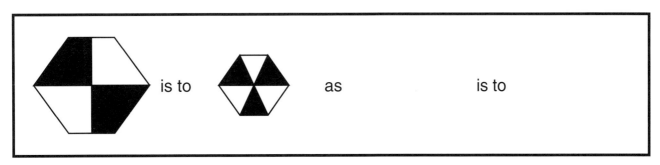

# Visual Figure-Ground

The tasks in this section provide practice perceiving and locating a form or object within a busy field. This skill is needed when trying to locate a screwdriver amidst other tools in the tool box, when trying to locate the tomato soup can amidst the many other varieties of soup cans on the supermarket shelf, or when trying to locate your car in a parking lot.

These tasks provide practice locating multiple items within the whole and locating a part within a whole. Both of these abilities are needed when using figure-ground skills to aid a person's visual reasoning abilities.

# Locating Items

The three shapes on the left are in the box on the right. The shapes will be the same size but may be rotated. Shade in each one you find.

# Locating Items

The items you will be looking for will be different sizes.

How many 2's are in this box?
Mark them.

Total = _____

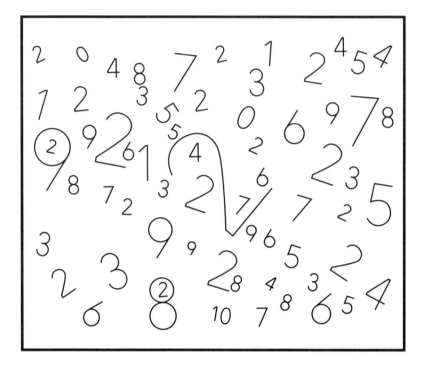

How many circles are in this box?
Mark them.

Total = _____

# Locating Items

The items you will be looking for will be different sizes.

How many S's are in this box?
Mark them.

Total = _____

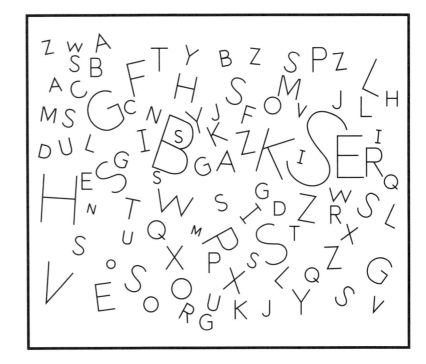

How many stars are in this box?
Mark them.

Total = _____

# Embedded Shapes

Look at the figures in the small boxes. Two of them are in the larger picture. Shade the shapes on the larger picture. The shapes will be the same size and won't be rotated.

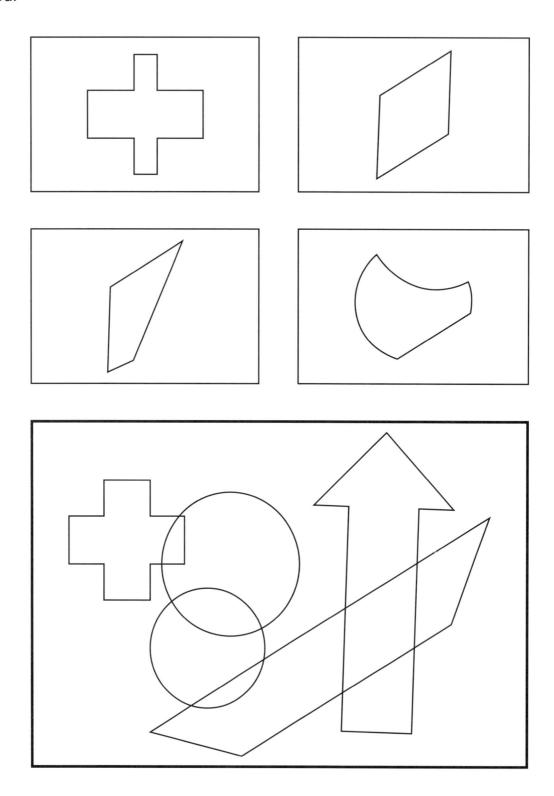

## Embedded Shapes

Look at the figures in the small boxes. Two of them are in the larger picture. Shade the shapes on the larger picture. The shapes will be the same size and won't be rotated.

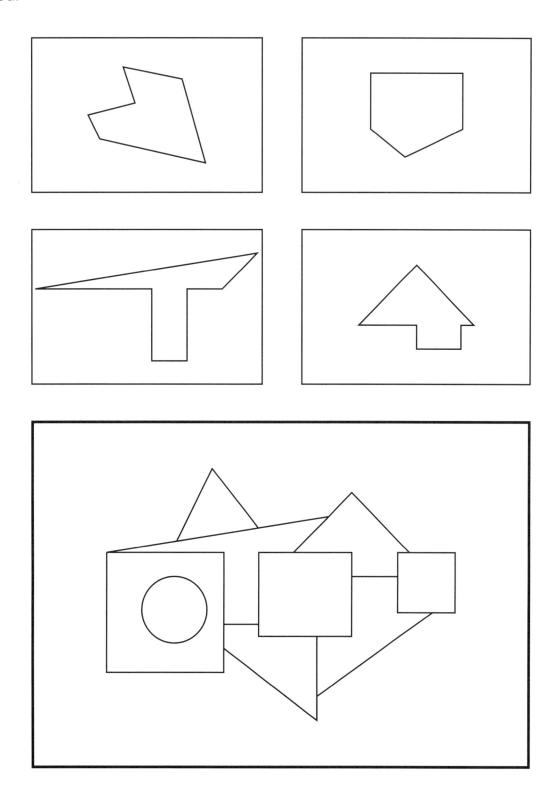

## Embedded Shapes

Look at the figures in the small boxes. Two of them are in the larger picture. Shade the shapes on the larger picture. The shapes will be the same size and won't be rotated.

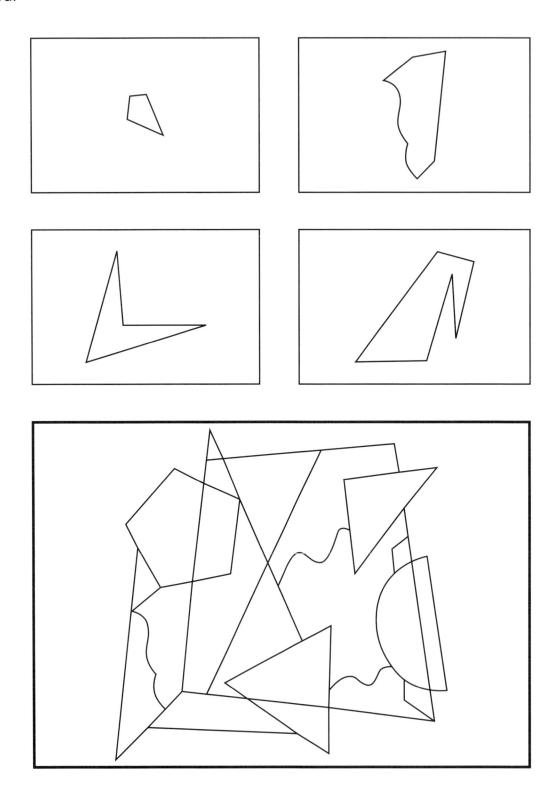

# Embedded Shapes

Look at the figures in the small boxes. Two of them are in the larger picture. Shade the shapes on the larger picture. The shapes will be the same size and won't be rotated.

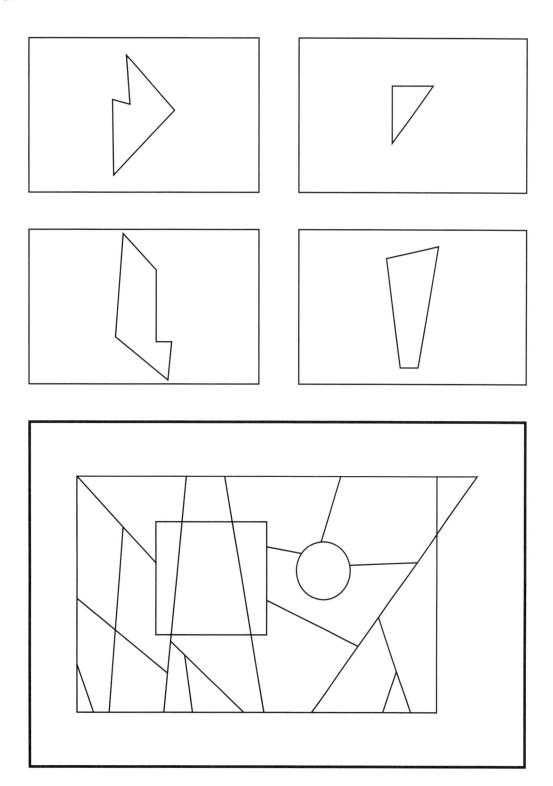

# Visual Sequencing

The tasks in this section address two different visual sequencing skills. The tasks in this section address two different visual sequencing skills.

1. Figural sequences that require your client to identify a progression of visual changes and then to use that deduction for providing the next item in a sequence.

2. Connect-the-dots activities that require your client to correctly sequence using different formats with the overlying picture content providing additional cues for successful visual reasoning. This task also stimulates the process of scanning ahead for anticipated visual stimuli in order to complete the task successfully.

The ability to determine and use a progression in visual stimuli is needed for such things as trying to determine what size pants a child may wear in a few months, determining how the weather may change from season to season, or knowing when and how things are growing in a vegetable garden. The ability to connect one object or picture to another to develop a successful visual plan is needed for such things as putting up a wallpaper border, setting a table, or arranging things on a shelf so they are aesthetically pleasing. Both of these skills are needed to make effective and logical reasoning decisions regarding visual sequencing.

# Figural Sequences—One Factor

Circle the shape that continues each sequence.

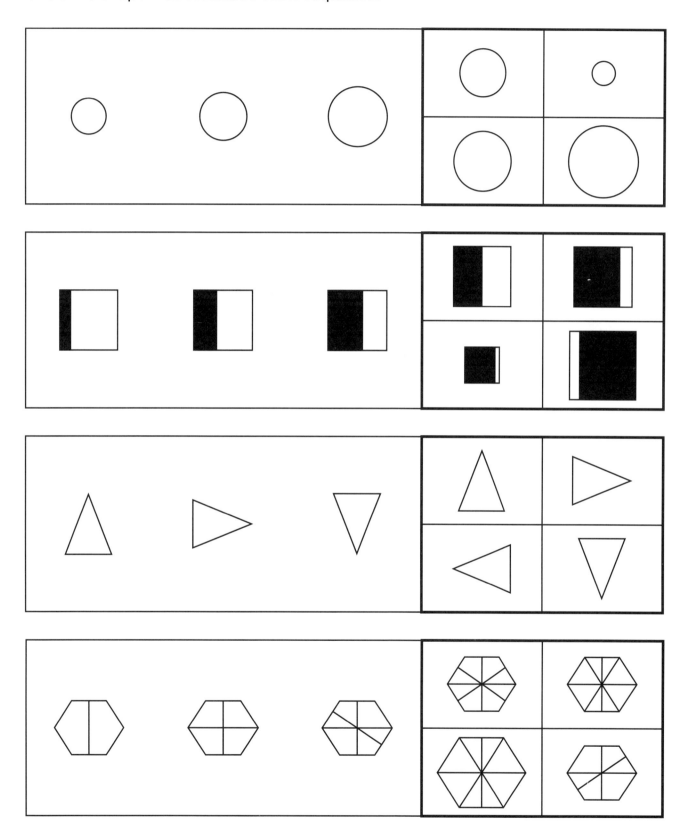

Visual Reasoning—Visual Sequencing
WALC 9: Verbal and Visual Reasoning

# Figural Sequences—One Factor

Draw the next shape in each sequence.

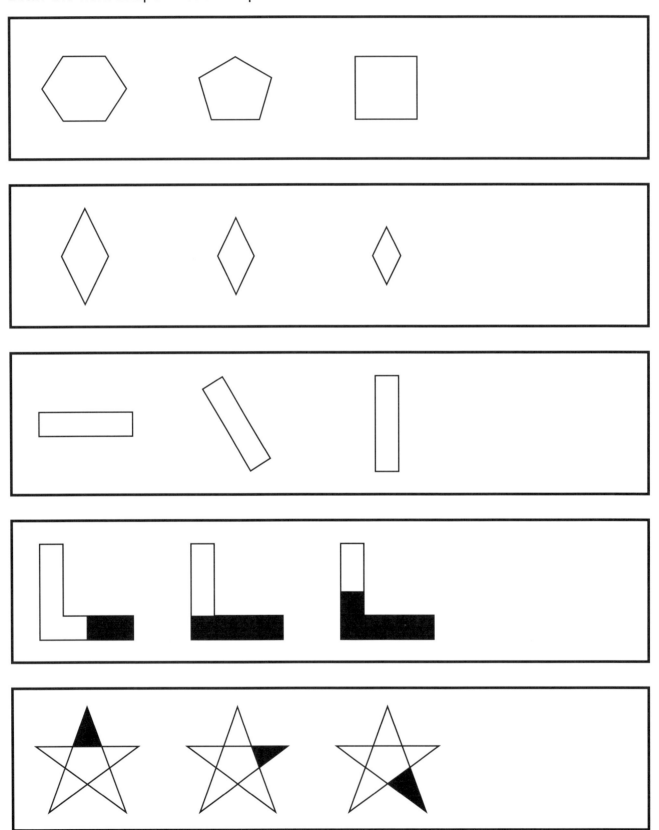

# Figural Sequences—Two Factors

Circle the shape that continues each sequence.

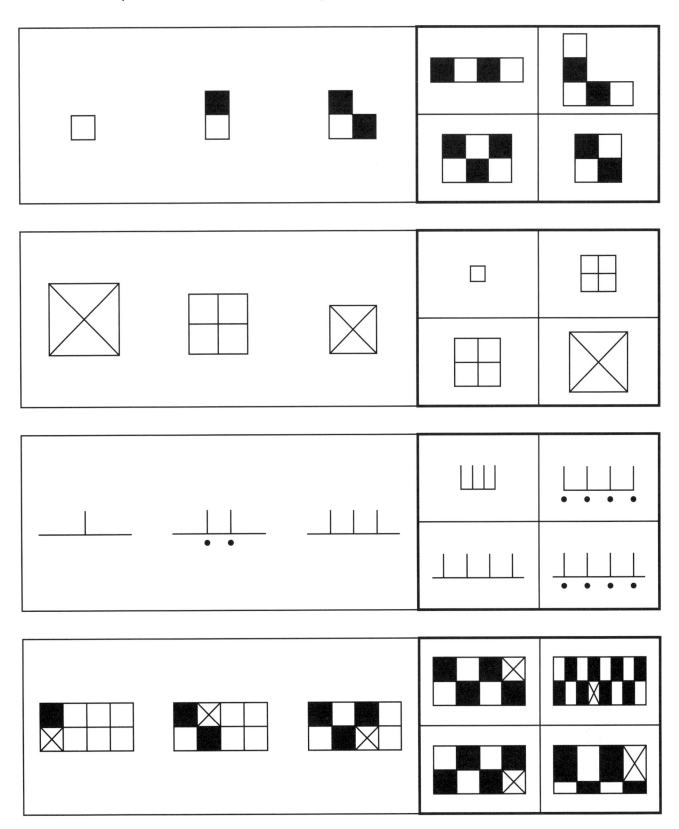

# Figural Sequences—Two Factors

Draw the next shape in each sequence.

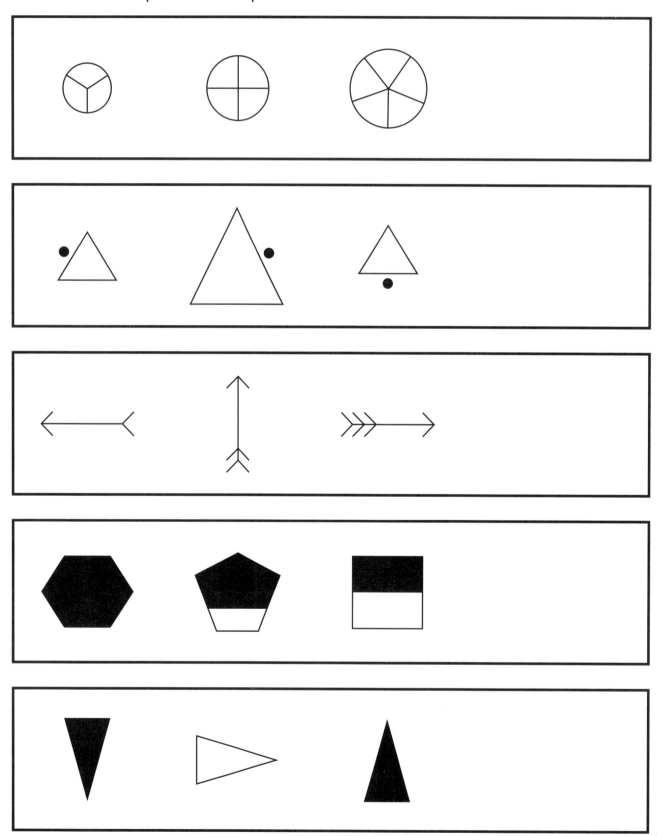

# Figural Sequences—Three Factors

Draw the next shape in each sequence.

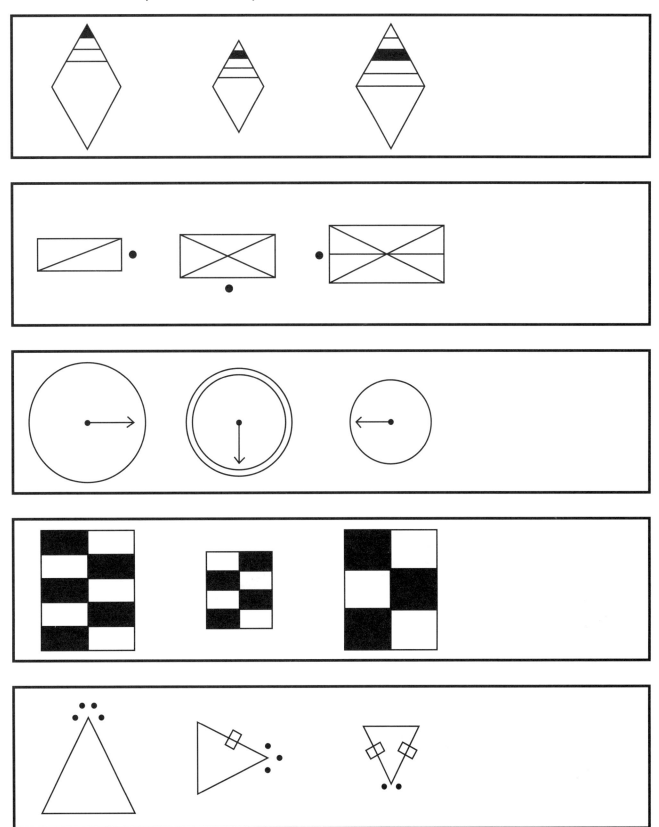

# Figural Sequences—Varying Number of Factors

Draw the next shape in each sequence.

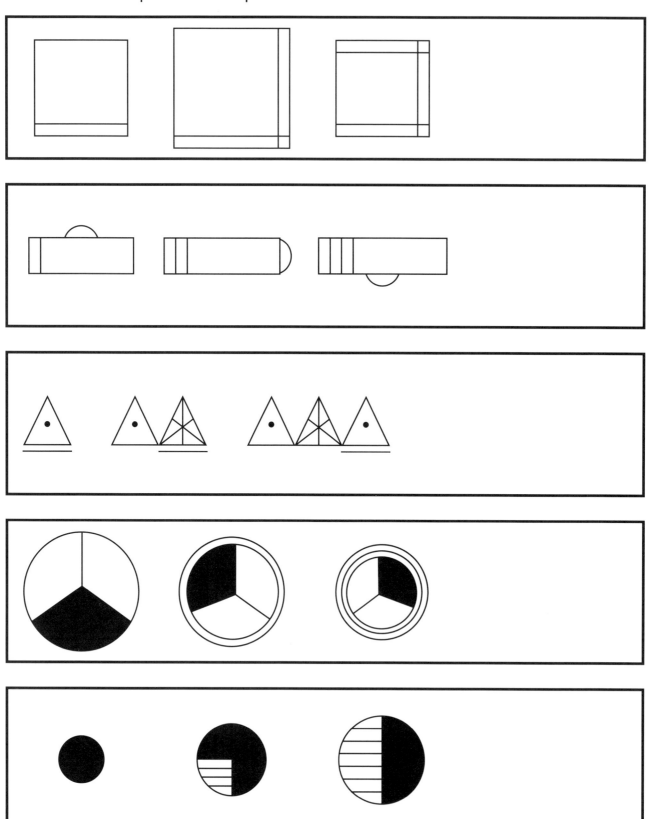

# Figural Sequences—Varying Number of Factors

Draw the next shape in each sequence.

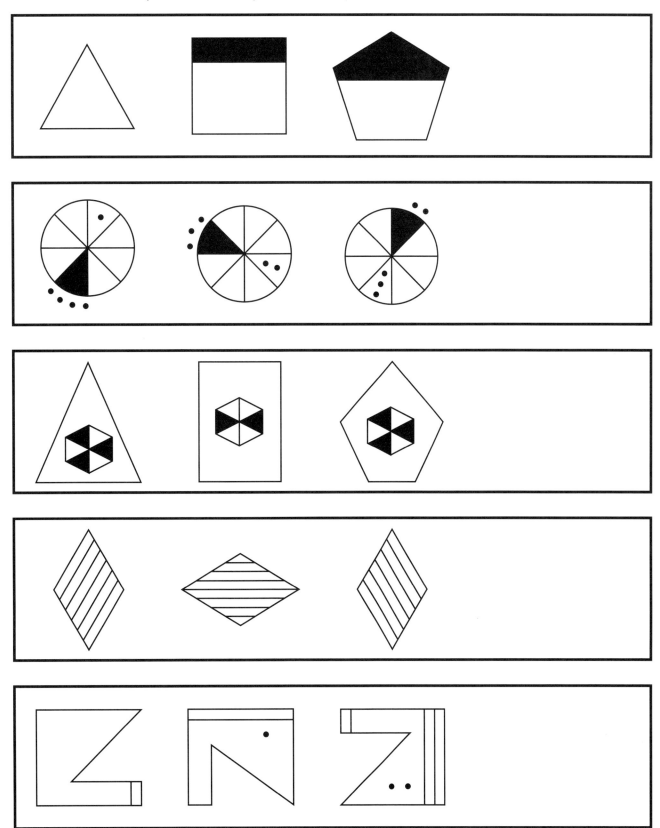

# Connect the Dots—Alphabetical

This connect-the-dots puzzle has pictures instead of numbers. Each picture begins with a different letter of the alphabet (A-R) and the letters are used once. Figure out what word each picture illustrates, then connect the dots in alphabetical order—starting with A. (Hint: A = arrow)

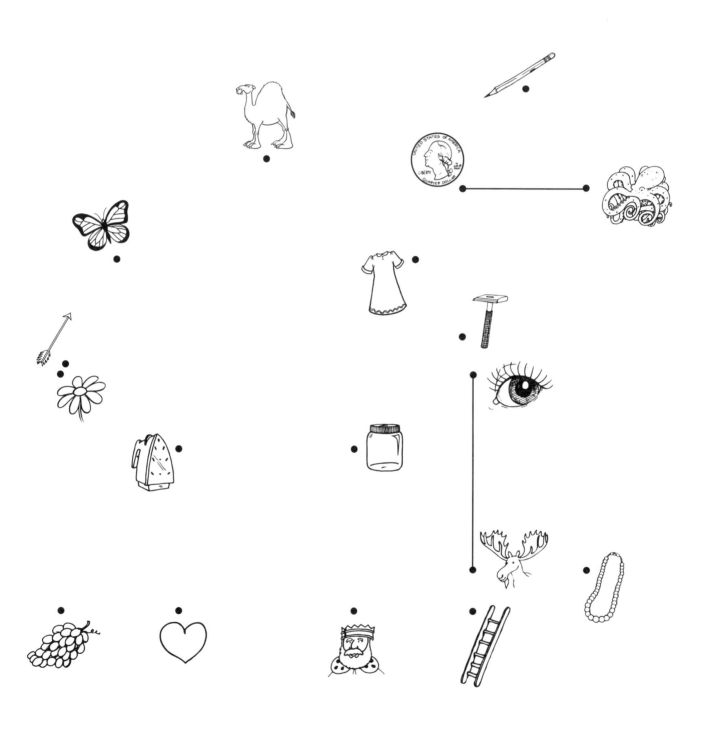

## Connect the Dots—Numerical

Connect the dots in order to make a picture. First try to visualize what the picture will be. Then start at 1 and connect one dot to the next without picking up your pencil. Try to scan ahead with your eyes and make a continuous movement.

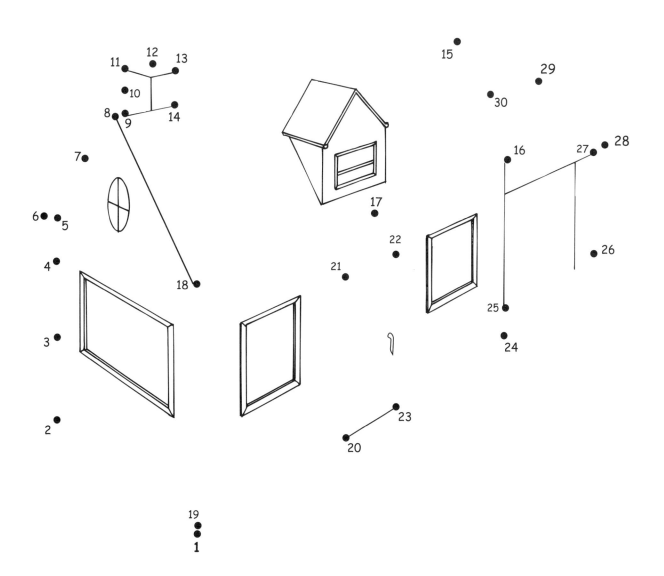

# Connect the Dots—Alternating

Connect the dots in order to make a picture. First try to visualize what the picture will be. Then start at 1 and connect one dot to the next without picking up your pencil. Try to scan ahead with your eyes and make a continuous movement.

Pattern: Connect the dots by alternating numbers and letters (1, A, 2, B, 3 . . .).

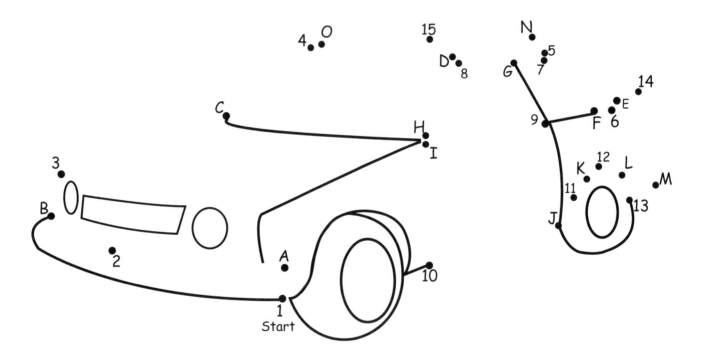

# Connect the Dots—Integration

Connect the dots in order to make a picture. First try to visualize what the picture will be. Begin at START and connect one dot to the next without picking up your pencil. Try to scan ahead with your eyes and make a continuous movement.

Pattern: Connect the dots to spell "This is for integration of cognitive skills."

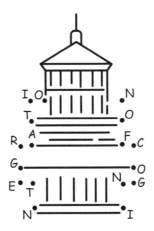

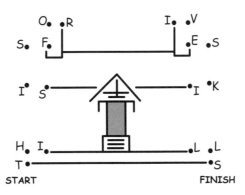

START                FINISH

# Visual Closure and Reasoning

The tasks in this section provide a variety of stimuli for your client to improve his visual closure and reasoning skills. Visual closure skills are needed to determine if visual stimuli is complete or if it is missing salient features. This skill is needed when scanning a check to insure that all blanks have been completed or to determine if all sections of a garden have been planted as mentally planned. Not only does your client need to determine completeness, he must have adequate visual reasoning skills to accurately fill in the missing information. These tasks address the identification and completion skills needed for effective visual closure.

The mirror images and figural grid activities add additional components to the visual reasoning tasks. When providing a mirror image, your client must reverse the information in order to draw the figure correctly. When completing the figural grid, your client must determine two different relationships (i.e., the actual figures used and what goes inside the figures) and determine the direction the relationship flows in the grid. These tasks will help your client improve his ability to manipulate factors which will lead to greater thought flexibility and more versatile reasoning skills.

When determining the differences between pictures, multiple processes become involved. Your client must be able to visually scan all quadrants of a picture and then compare that stored information to a visually similar picture. In addition, your client will anticipate possibilities for what he feels might be changed and then visually reason and compare to determine if his thoughts were correct. These types of skills are needed for a variety of daily activities, such as scanning a dinner table to determine if all needed items are on the table as well as realizing that differences will occur from one night to the next.

The picture inference tasks will help your client interpret visual stimuli which leads to making an inferential decision. Your client needs to be able to interpret what he sees and to make fact-based deductions about the information in order to have effective visual reasoning skills.

The picture tasks with false information will help your client identify when incongruities are being presented. This skill is needed for determining when an error might have been written in instructions or in a recipe, when dressing and making sure your socks match and only one sweater is worn, or when trying to decide what is factual verses inferential information presented in an advertisement.

# Closure

Circle the shape that completes each square.

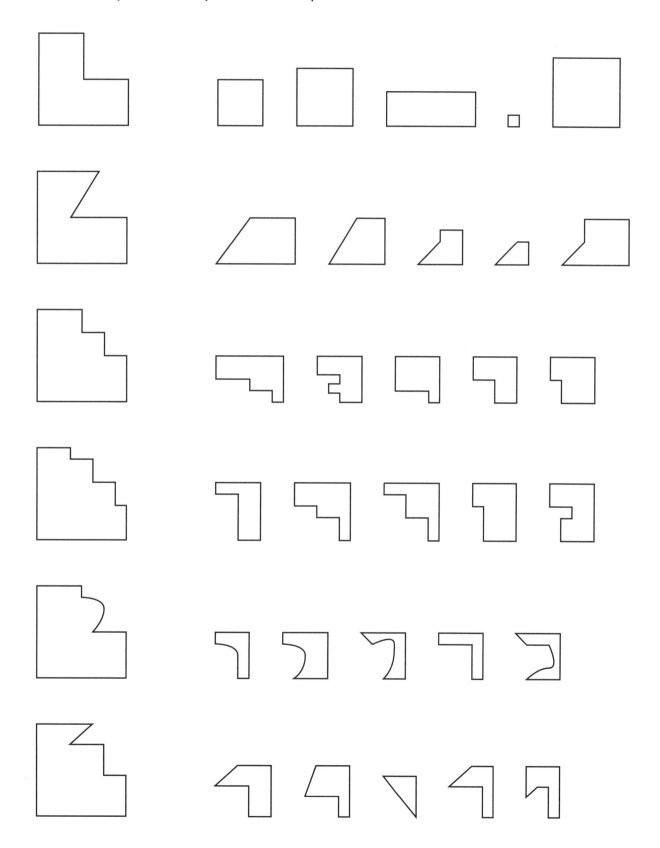

# Closure

Circle the shape that completes each square.

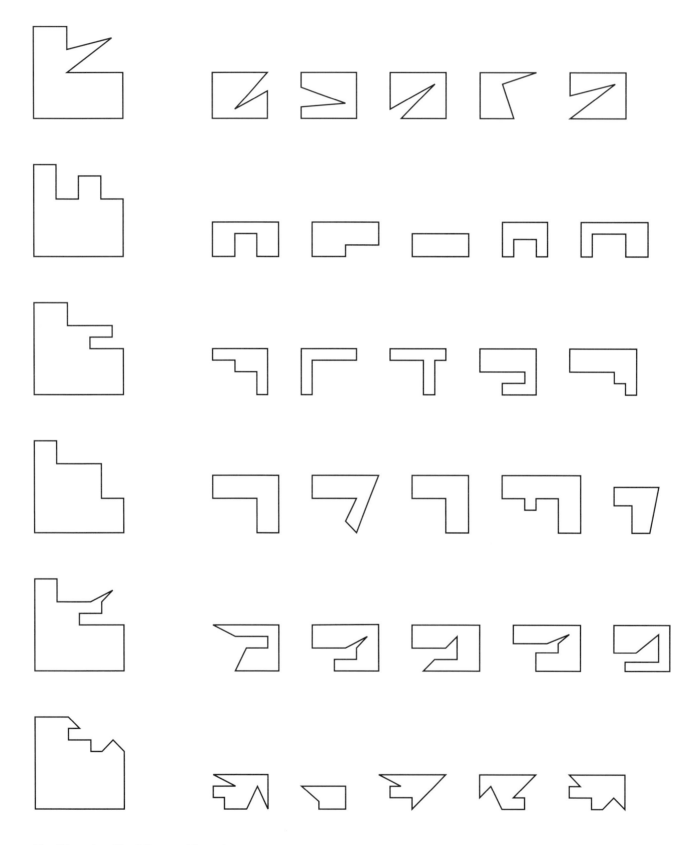

# Mirror Images

Draw the mirror image for each picture.

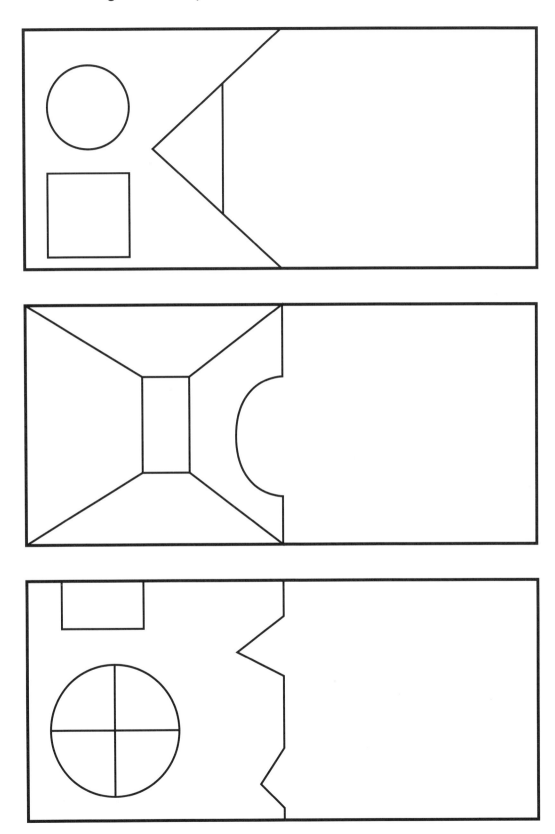

## Mirror Images

Draw the mirror image for each picture.

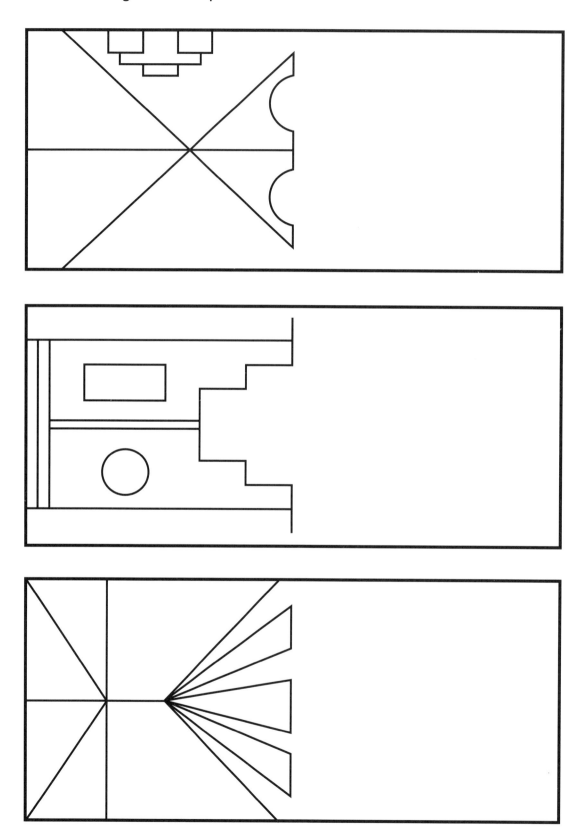

# Figural Grid

Complete each grid. There is one thing that is the same for the items across each row. There will also be one thing the same down each row. Each grid will have different factors.

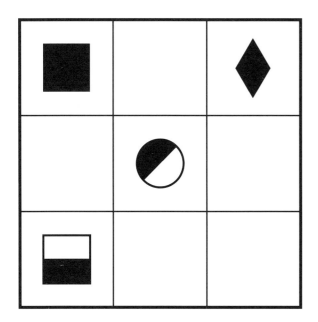

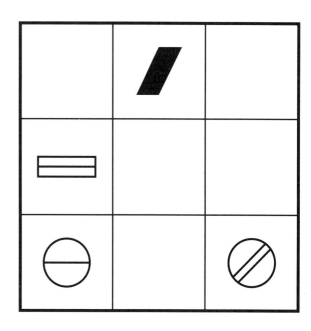

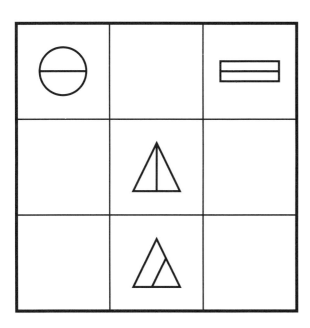

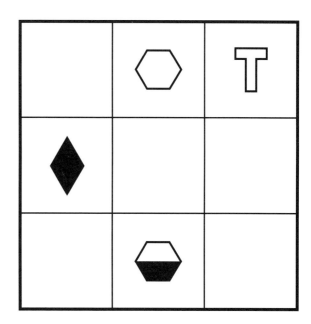

# Figural Grid

Complete each grid. There must be one thing that is the same for the items across each row. There will also be one thing the same down each row. Each grid will have different factors.

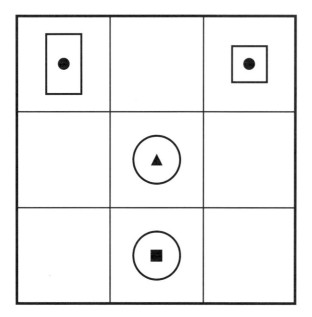
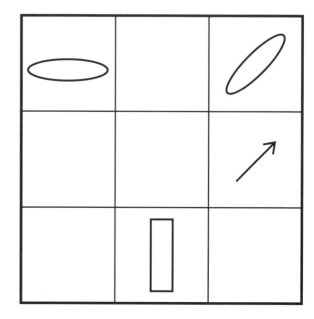
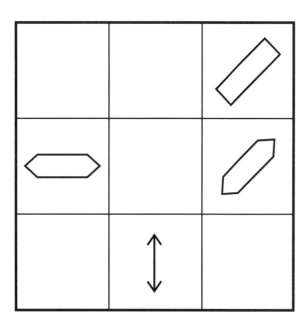
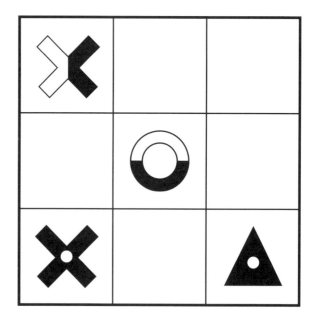

# Differences Between Pictures

Locate at least 10 differences between the pictures.

# Differences Between Pictures

Locate at least 10 differences between the pictures.

# Differences Between Pictures

Locate at least 10 differences between the pictures.

# Differences Between Pictures

Locate at least 10 differences between the pictures.

# Picture Inferences

Answer the question about each picture.

What might have caused the plant to wilt?

Why might the man be taking his dog here?

What is this couple doing?

Why isn't this deli open for business?

## Picture Inferences

Answer the questions about each picture.

Why might the police officer have stopped this car?

What time of day is it? How do you know?

How might this woman have gotten a flat tire?

Why might this man be upset? What do you think will happen next?

## Picture Inferences

Answer the questions about each picture.

Why might this girl have mixed feelings about her report card?

What problem do you think this couple is having? How can you tell?

Why do you think this boy is in bed? How do you know?

Why might the dog be looking at an empty dish?

# Picture Inferences

Answer the questions about each picture.

Why might this man be crawling under the bed?

What is about to happen? What will the cat do? What will the boy do?

What is happening? Why is this happening?

Why is this woman running after the bus?

# Picture Incongruities

Identify what doesn't make sense in each picture.

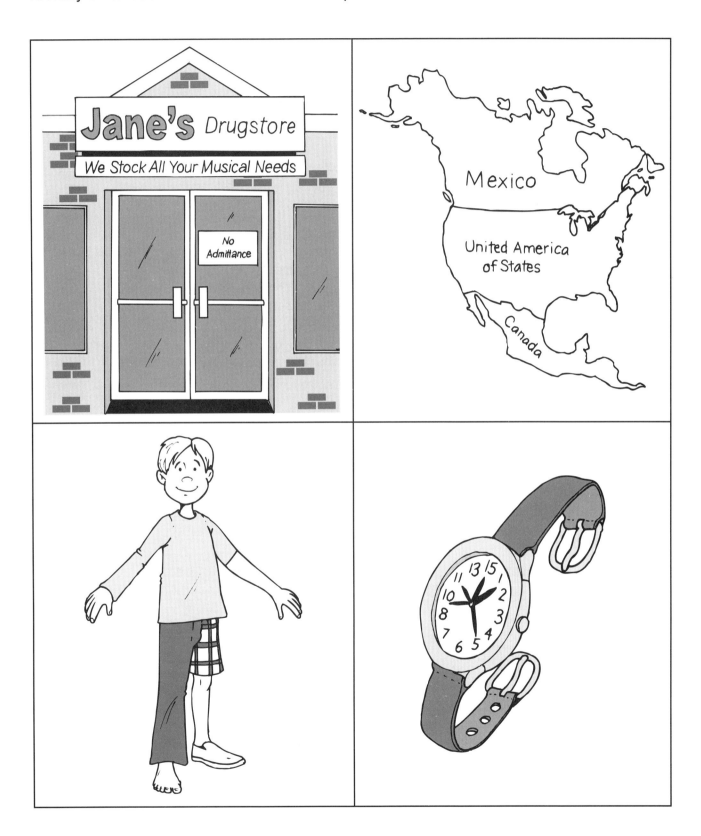

# Picture Incongruities

Identify what doesn't make sense in each picture.

Visual Reasoning—Visual Closure and Reasoning
WALC 9: Verbal and Visual Reasoning

# Picture Incongruities

Identify what doesn't make sense in each picture.

# Drawing

The three tasks in this section are very high level and require multiple levels of visual reasoning, including organization and the ability to mentally manipulate visual plans in your head. These tasks should be used with clients who have a specific need for this type of visual task (e.g., architect, engineer, interior designer). The tasks involve multiple levels of deduction and visual planning which can help your client be successful in his job.

## Directions—Grid

Sketch out Kathy's vacation route on the grid. Then answer the questions.

Starting from the beach house (B), she travels 4 miles south to the beach, then 5 miles east to the boat dock, 2 miles north to the souvenir store, then 3 miles west to Arthur's Seafood Restaurant, and 2 miles north to pick up the kids from the miniature golf course. From there, she goes directly home to the beach house.

Note: Each square equals one mile.

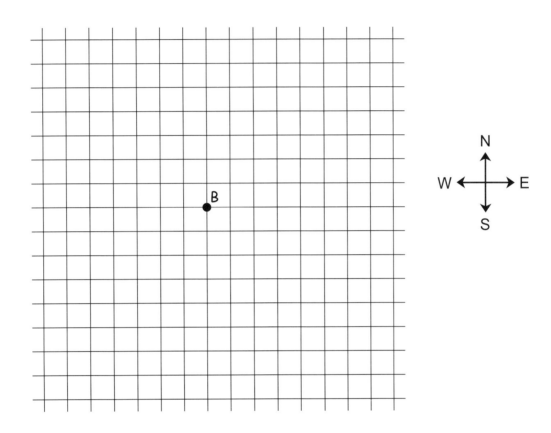

1. How far is the beach house from the miniature golf course?

2. In which direction did Kathy travel to go directly home to the beach house from the miniature golf course?

3. How long was the total route?

# Draw Figure to Scale

Draw the railroad crossing sign to scale on the grid provided. It is recommended that you start at the base and work upward.

Note: Each square equals 6 square inches.

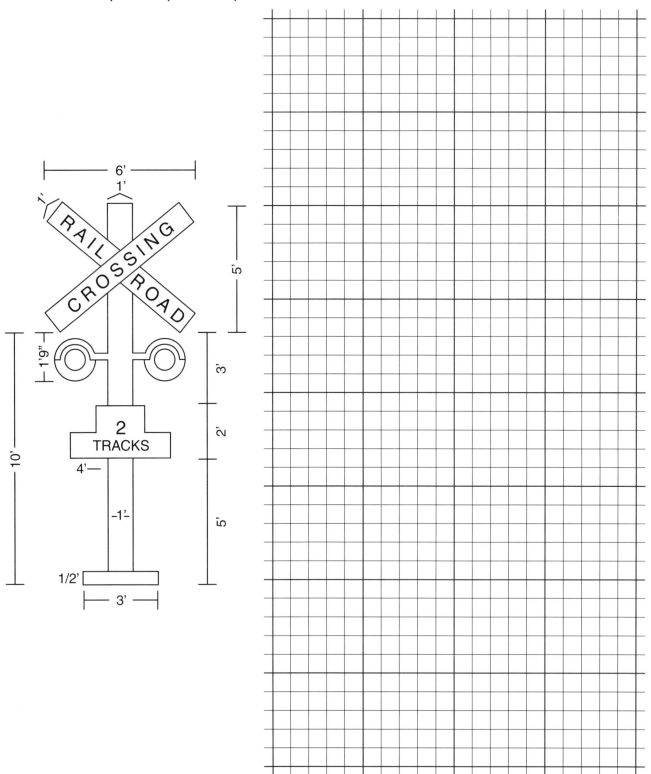

*Visual Reasoning—Drawing*
*WALC 9: Verbal and Visual Reasoning*

# Floor Plan Sketch

Using the grid on the next page, sketch a floor plan of a living room. It must include all of the following items. Make sure that you make it proportional. There are multiple ways it can be done, so design the room however you want.

Note: Each square equals 6 square inches.

Items to include:

Size of room: 16 feet by 20 feet (16' x 20')

Windows:
1. Bay window – 6' wide; it has a 9" windowsill that juts into the room.
2. One window – 3' wide.

Doors:
There are two doorways leading to other parts of the house; each is 3' wide.

Furniture:
1. Sofa is 6½' long and 3' wide.
2. Recliner is 3 square feet when not extended – 5' when extended.
3. Two end tables are 2' x 2'.
4. One floor lamp – its base is 9" in diameter.
5. Entertainment Center is 6' x 3'.
6. Bookshelf is 4' x 1½'.
7. Two table lamps are average size.
8. Magazine rack is 1' x 1½'.
9. Straight-back chair is 1½' x 1½'.
10. Coffee table is 5' x 2'.

# Floor Plan Sketch

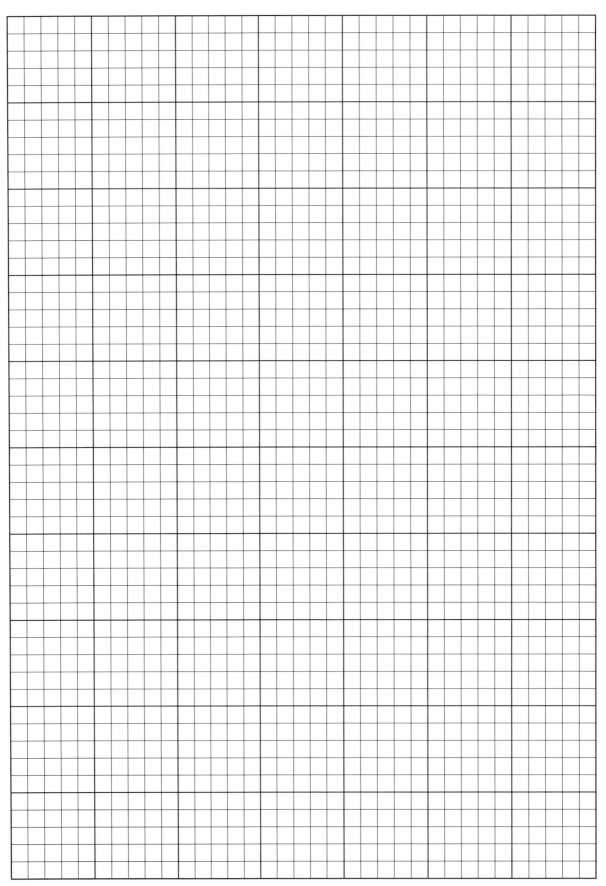

# Resources

▶ **Evidence-Based Research Articles Regarding Therapy for Cognitive-Communication Disorders**

American Speech-Language-Hearing Association. (2006). *Treatment efficacy summary: Aphasia resulting from left hemisphere stroke.* Retrieved 12/23/06 from www.asha.org.

American Speech-Language-Hearing Association. (2006). *Treatment efficacy summary: Cognitive-communication disorders resulting from right hemisphere brain damage.* Retrieved 12/23/06 from www.asha.org.

American Speech-Language-Hearing Association. (2006). *Treatment efficacy summary: Cognitive-communication disorders resulting from traumatic brain injury.* Retrieved 12/23/06 from www.asha.org.

Boghal, S.K., Teasell, R.W., Foley, N.C., & Speechley, M.R. (2003). Rehabilitation of aphasia: More is better. *Topics in Stroke Rehabilitation, 10(2)*, 66-76.

Carney, N., Chestnut, R., Maynard, H., Mann, N.C., Patterson, P., & Helfand, M. (1999). Effect of cognitive rehabilitation on outcomes for persons with traumatic brain injury: A systematic review. *Journal of Head Trauma Research, 14(3)*, 277-307.

Cicerone, K.D., Dahlberg, C., Kalmar, K., Langenbahn, D.M., Malec, J., Bergquist, T.F., et al. (2000). Evidence-based cognitive rehabilitation: Recommendations for clinical practice. *Archives of Physical Medicine and Rehabilitation, 81(12)*, 1596-1615.

Cicerone, K.D., Dahlberg, C., Malec, J., Langenbahn, D.M., Felicetti, T., Kneipp, S., et al. (2005). Evidence-based cognitive rehabilitation: Updated review of the literature from 1998 through 2002. *Archives of Physical Medicine and Rehabilitation, 86(8)*, 1681-1692.

Coelho, C.A., DeRuyter, F., & Stein, M. (1996). Treatment efficacy: Cognitive-communication disorders resulting from traumatic brain injury in adults. *Journal of Speech and Hearing Research, 39(5)*, S5-S17.

Winocur, G., Craik, F.I.M., Levine, B., Robertson, I.H., Binns, M.A., Alexander, M., et al. (2007). Cognitive rehabilitation in the elderly: Overview and future directions. *Journal of the International Neuropsychological Society, 13*, 166-171.

▶ **Books**

Elman, R. (Ed.). (2006). *Group treatment of neurogenic communication disorders: The expert clinician's approach. (2nd ed.).* San Diego: Plural Publishing, Inc.

Helms-Estabrooks, N., & Albert, M.L. (2005). *Manual of aphasia and aphasia therapy.* Austin, TX: Pro-Ed, Inc.

Hillis, A. (2002). *The handbook of adult language disorders.* NY: Psychology Press, an imprint of the Taylor & Francis Group.

Keith, R.L., & Schumacher, J.G. (2001). *Speech and language rehabilitation. (4th ed.).* Austin, TX: Pro-Ed, Inc.

LaPointe, L.L. (2005). *Aphasia and related neurogenic language disorders. (3rd ed.).* NYC: Thieme Publishers.

Sarno, M.T., & Peters, J.F. (Eds). (2004). *The aphasia handbook: A guide for stroke and brain injury survivors and their families.* NYC: National Aphasia Association.

## ▶ Organizations

### American Speech-Language-Hearing Association (ASHA)
Promotes the interests of and provides the highest quality services for professionals in audiology, speech-language pathology, and speech and hearing science; advocates for people with communication disabilities

*www.asha.org*
Action Center: 800-498-2071 (members); 800-638-8255 (non-members)

### Aphasia Hope Foundation
Promotes research into the prevention and cure of aphasia as well as insuring that all survivors of aphasia and their caregivers are aware of and have access to the best possible treatments available; the largest collaborative online resource for aphasia

*www.aphasiahope.org*
866-449-5804 (toll free)

### Brain Injury Association of America (BIA)
Provides information, education, and support to persons currently living with TBI, their families, and professionals working with individuals who have sustained a TBI

*www.biausa.org*
800-444-6443

### National Aphasia Association (NAA)
Promotes public education, research, rehabilitation, and support services to assist people with aphasia and their families

*www.aphasia.org*
800-922-4622

### National Institute of Neurological Disorders & Stroke (NINDS)
Supports and conducts research on the brain and nervous system; fosters the training of investigators in the basic and clinical neurosciences; and seeks better understanding, diagnosis, treatment, and prevention of neurological disorders

*www.ninds.nih.gov*
800-352-9424

### National Rehabilitation Information Center (NARIC)
Provides information to the disability and rehabilitation community through online publications, searchable databases, and timely reference and referral data

*www.naric.com*
800-346-2742

### National Stroke Association (NSA)
Provides information and resources for stroke survivors, their families, and caregivers

*www.stroke.org*
800-787-6537 (STROKES)

## ▶ Websites for Clients

*www.happyneuron.com*
This website provides entertaining and challenging games that are fun and scientifically-developed to keep your brain fit. This is a subscription-based website but free trials are available.

*www.queendom.com*
This website includes psychological tests, just-for-fun tests, mind games, and puzzles.

# Answer Key

The most likely answers are listed here. Accept other logical, appropriate answers as correct.

**page 11**
Answers will vary.

**page 12**
1. excited
2. depressed
3. nervous
4. proud
5. frustrated
6. ecstatic
7. confident
8. lonely
9. anxious
10. scared
11. worried, scared
12. panicked, scared
13. ashamed, guilty
14. content
15. nervous, curious
16. joyous
17. embarrassed
18. bored
19. lonely
20. anxious

**pages 13-26**
Answers will vary.

**page 27**
1. True
2. False
3. True
4. True
5. True
6. False
7. False
8. True
9. True

**page 28**
1. Rambles
2. Gets to the point
3. Rambles
4. Rambles
5. Gets to the point

**page 29**
1. Excluding
2. Including
3. Including
4. Excluding
5. Excluding
6. Excluding
7. Including

**page 30**
1. Open
2. Argumentative
3. Argumentative
4. Open
5. Argumentative
6. Open
7. Argumentative
8. Argumentative

**page 31**
1. Attentive
2. Bored
3. Attentive
4. Bored
5. Bored
6. Attentive
7. Bored
8. Attentive
9. Attentive
10. Bored
11. Bored
12. Attentive

**page 32**
1. Do
2. Don't
3. Do
4. Don't
5. Don't
6. Do
7. Don't
8. Do
9. Don't

**page 33**
1. Tactful
2. Offensive
3. Offensive
4. Tactful
5. Offensive
6. Tactful
7. Offensive
8. Offensive
9. Tactful
10. Tactful
11. Offensive

**page 34**
1. Stop
2. Stop
3. Encourage
4. Encourage
5. Stop
6. Encourage
7. Encourage
8. Stop
9. Stop
10. Encourage

**page 35**
Topics will vary.
1. Wait
2. Start
3. Start
4. Start
5. Wait
6. Wait

**pages 37-40**
Explanation of expressions will vary.

**page 37**
1. keeps the doctor away
2. is a penny earned
3. all wounds
4. are soon parted
5. is worth two in the bush
6. on the other side
7. for the trees
8. the best policy
9. than water
10. skin a cat
11. heart grow fonder
12. a friend indeed
13. angels fear to tread
14. before they're hatched
15. his mouth
16. the root of all evil
17. by its cover
18. spoil the broth
19. a man healthy, wealthy, and wise
20. in one basket

**page 38**
1. eat it too
2. you leap
3. new tricks
4. in a haystack
5. waste
6. golden
7. all trades
8. better than one
9. from a stone, from a turnip
10. a silver lining
11. than never
12. flock together
13. spilled milk
14. the cat
15. the mice will play
16. the golden egg
17. be choosers
18. laughs best
19. out of a molehill
20. louder than words

**page 39**
1. jack of all trades
2. A friend in need is a friend indeed.
3. chip off the old block
4. Time will tell.
5. Where there's a will, there's a way.
6. Too many cooks spoil the broth.
7. Two heads are better than one.
8. A stitch in time saves nine.
9. Two wrongs don't make a right.
10. Rolling stones gather no moss.
11. Necessity is the mother of all invention.
12. A fool and his money are soon parted.
13. You can't have your cake and eat it too.
14. can't see the forest for the trees
15. There are other fish in the sea.

**page 40**
2. tongue
3. stomach
4. chest
5. eyes
6. leg
7. nose
8. foot
9. head
10. shoulder
11. head
12. mouth
13. face
14. elbow
15. stomach

**page 41**
2. She has a live frog in her throat. She has a hoarse voice.

3. The cup of tea on the table is not mine. That's not something I like to do.
4. He threw a stone and killed two birds. He got two things done at the same time.
5. Leave the sleeping dogs alone. Don't get people riled up; leave things as they are.
6. Her husband sat in the back seat to drive. Her husband told her how to drive as she was driving.

**page 42**
2. You should take something off your chest. You should talk about what is bothering you.
3. She wrapped his body around her finger. He did everything she said.
4. He has a poker chip balanced on his shoulder. He thinks he's better than everyone.
5. She should dig a hole and bury a hatchet in it. She should make amends.
6. His eyes were really big. He took more food than he could eat.

**page 43**
2. All shiny things are not gold. Something may not be as good as it looks.
3. You can take the skin off a cat in more than one way. There is more than one way to do something.
4. Eat an apple every day and you won't have to see a doctor. Eating healthy food will keep you fit and you won't have to see a doctor.
5. The grass in your neighbor's yard is greener than your grass. Other people's situations always look better.
6. You can't teach an old dog to do a new trick. You can't change someone.

**page 44**
1. d
2. i
3. g
4. k
5. a
6. h
7. b
8. l
9. c
10. j
11. e
12. f

**page 46**
1. coal, tar
2. truck, mountain
3. tea
4. car, house
5. apple, tomato
6. ball
7. people, cars
8. bubble, balloon
9. stick, glass
10. dog, cat, car
11. person, tree
12. grass, hair
13. cat
14. floor
15. cheese
16. people
17. boat
18. people, plants
19. subscription, insurance
20. cake, hard-boiled egg

**page 47**
1. rope, snake, speech
2. refrigerator
3. elbow, straw
4. car, hose
5. ice, fish
6. diamond, jewelry
7. blanket
8. stars
9. apple, shirt, markers
10. knife, pencil
11. airplane, helicopter
12. square, rectangle, desk
13. teeth, license
14. chair, table
15. glass, window
16. cell phone, video camera
17. tortoise, tree
18. newborn, cat
19. turtle, frog
20. helicopter

**page 48**
1. bird
2. tablecloth
3. water
4. suitcase, box
5. plants, people
6. rubber band
7. choir, wedding
8. pen, newspaper, candy
9. sponge
10. sky, colors
11. hair
12. sneakers, shirt, cat
13. money, wallet, keys
14. log, sponge, person
15. ping-pong ball
16. soda pop, juice
17. people, animals
18. refrigerator, TV, computer
19. video games
20. driving

**pages 49-52**
Answers will vary.

**page 53**
1. plain
2. sticky
3. reduce
4. spiral
5. limit
6. ruler
7. fighting
8. theorize
9. voice
10. question
11. shocking
12. jealousy
13. attend
14. basement
15. pyramid
16. awful
17. math
18. whine
19. schedule
20. dirt

**page 54**
1. joke
2. oven
3. whim
4. return
5. impish
6. slow
7. show
8. horror
9. imagine
10. snap
11. disgusted
12. square
13. draw
14. wait
15. visitation
16. book
17. silver
18. increase
19. steel
20. ticket

**page 55**
2. dogs
3. toys
4. fruit
5. TV shows
6. colors
7. residences
8. trees
9. clothing
10. vehicles
11. footwear
12. body parts
13. musical instruments
14. silverware
15. animals

**page 56**
2. candy
3. kitchen appliances
4. pants
5. gymnastics
6. bright/light colors
7. precipitation
8. beans
9. wild animals
10. tables
11. plays, movies
12. facial features
13. pain relievers
14. brass instruments
15. jewelry

**page 57**
2. soda pop
3. bee, hornet, yellow jacket, wasp
4. salt, pepper
5. diamond, topaz
6. racket
7. dog, cat
8. *Hello, Dolly!*, *The Sound of Music*
9. sneakers, tennis shoes
10. spring, summer, fall, winter
11. happy
12. Honda, Toyota
13. cheddar, Swiss
14. ambulance, fire truck
15. dandelion

**page 58**
car
pets
kitchen appliances
things to read
outerwear
birds
Target, Wal-Mart
colors
rain
winter sports
writing implements

**page 59**
weeds
vegetables
duck
body parts
garden tools
chicken pox
sports
NyQuil, cough syrup
food
TV shows
Earth, Mars

**page 60**
2. animal, bear, polar bear
3. medical profession, doctor, podiatrist
4. dairy, cheeses, extra-sharp cheddar
5. toys, construction toys, Lincoln Logs
6. dogs, sporting dogs, Labrador retrievers
7. literature, novels, *Gone With the Wind*
8. transportation, air transportation, jet
9. vacation spot, national parks, Yellowstone
10. flowers, spring bloomers, tulips
11. entertainment, video game, *Search the Mountain*
12. furniture, chairs, rocking chairs

**page 62**
1. O
2. F
3. F
4. O
5. F
6. O
7. O
8. F
9. O
10. F
11. F
12. O
13. O
14. F
15. O

**page 63**
1. O
2. F
3. F
4. O
5. O
6. F
7. O
8. F
9. F
10. O
11. O
12. F
13. O
14. F
15. O

**page 64**
1. F
2. T
3. F
4. F
5. F
6. T
7. T
8. F
9. T
10. F
11. F
12. F
13. T
14. F
15. T
16. T
17. F
18. T
19. F
20. T

**page 65**
1. F
2. T
3. T
4. F
5. T
6. F
7. F
8. T
9. F
10. T
11. T
12. F
13. T
14. T
15. F
16. T
17. T
18. F
19. F
20. T

**page 66**
1. Sunday, Tuesday, Friday
2. yesterday, today, tomorrow
3. second, minute, hour
4. year, decade, century
5. order, eat, pay or order, pay, eat
6. pack, depart, arrive
7. kindergarten, junior high, high school
8. caterpillar, cocoon, butterfly
9. shuffle, deal, play, win
10. seed, sprout, bud, blossom
11. bait, cast, catch, clean
12. lose, search, find
13. read, memorize, test
14. January, May, August, October
15. dream, plan, build, occupy

**page 67**
1. cool, cold, freezing
2. daughter, mother, grandmother
3. walk, jog, sprint
4. least, less, more, most
5. glance, look, stare
6. whimper, cry, sob
7. rare, medium, well-done
8. warm, simmer, boil
9. bothered, angry, furious
10. private, sergeant, general
11. silent, quiet, loud
12. negative, neutral, positive
13. lower, middle, upper
14. suspect, investigate, convict
15. tiny, small, large, giant

**page 68**
1. silence, whisper, talk, shout
2. grin, giggle, laugh, guffaw
3. shed, cabin, house, mansion
4. dark, dim, bright, brilliant
5. near, far, farther, farthest
6. drop, trickle, flow, gush
7. mayor, governor, president
8. sad, content, glad, joyous
9. town, state, nation, continent
10. hideous, ugly, plain, pretty
11. ancient, old, present, futuristic
12. impossible, possible, probable, definite
13. fast, snack, meal, feast
14. white, ivory, gray, black
15. minute, small, medium, large

**page 69**
1. inside
2. trace
3. tender
4. that
5. creamy
6. oatmeal
7. starfish
8. tactful
9. useful
10. vanilla
11. drags
12. done
13. space
14. growing
15. tone
16. shots
17. colder
18. police
19. pancake
20. items
21. touchdown
22. hanging
23. meeting
24. camel
25. crank
26. everyone
27. maiden
28. changed
29. apart
30. damage

**page 70**
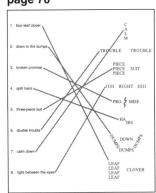

**page 71**

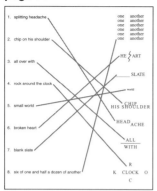

**page 72**

**page 73**
read between the lines
forgive and forget
backhand
long underwear
sandbox
buckle up for safety
foot in the door
I understand
tricycle
high school

**page 74**
downstairs
crossroads
blank check
wish upon a star
monkey in the middle
turn of the century
ship overseas
upset, set up
split level
three square meals

**page 75**
1. tale
2. page
3. team
4. plate
5. brag
6. ever
7. tape
8. fear
9. dogs
10. file
11. eat
12. form
13. care
14. east, eats
15. tone
16. ripe
17. name
18. table
19. stop
20. news
21. field
22. idea
23. ride
24. march
25. free
26. horse
27. rise
28. send, dens
29. robe
30. tire

**page 76**
1. mile
2. stale, steal
3. skit
4. capes
5. feat
6. came
7. thing
8. gear
9. deal
10. lose
11. face
12. rule
13. thermos, smother
14. north
15. diet, tied
16. add
17. room
18. rate
19. sure
20. cheap
21. these
22. gates
23. draw
24. tapes
25. part
26. pace
27. beard, bared
28. open, nope
29. stake, steak, takes
30. teach

**page 77**
1. time
2. parts
3. bread
4. tea
5. peach
6. race
7. palm
8. skate
9. cheat
10. north
11. salt
12. ride
13. meat
14. east
15. from

**page 78**
1. reef
2. shore
3. lead
4. sheet
5. pots
6. shrub
7. night
8. gear
9. much
10. robe
11. mane
12. idea
13. fare
14. pierce
15. quiet

**page 79**
1. colony
2. periodical
3. commandment
4. sweetheart
5. percentage
6. equality
7. surplus
8. bandage
9. center
10. starboard
11. pint
12. Times Square

**page 80**
1. starch
2. percentile
3. pinch
4. colonial
5. plush
6. heartburn
7. centipede
8. commander
9. periodic
10. android
11. equally
12. New York Times

**page 81**
1. orange, green, yellow
2. gold, silver, copper
3. corn, peas, pumpkin
4. couch, chair, table
5. year, hour, month
6. river, creek, gulf
7. book, letter, note
8. shirt, jacket, slacks
9. shoe, boot, slipper
10. snake, turtle, toad
11. milk, soda, tea
12. dog, cat, fish
13. arm, foot, ankle
14. month, day, week
15. one, five, forty

**page 82**
1. lime, cherry, grape
2. brush, comb, curlers
3. glue, tape, staple
4. truck, car, van
5. branch, twig, stick
6. train, plane, bus
7. salt, pepper, clove
8. touch, hear, smell
9. tack, nail, bolt
10. wood, log, stick
11. golf, track, biking or hiking
12. face, neck, chin
13. bowl, dish, glass
14. door, wall, floor
15. rain, hail, snow

**page 83**
Answers will vary.

**page 84**
1. 7 days of the week
2. 52 cards in a deck
3. 12 months in a year
4. 50 states in the United States
5. 60 minutes in an hour
6. 18 holes on a golf course
7. 4 quarters in a dollar
8. 3 sides on a triangle
9. 52 weeks in a year
10. 9 players on a baseball team
11. 24 hours in a day
12. 36 inches in a yard
13. 100 years in a century
14. 2 pints in a quart
15. 365 days in a year

**page 85**
a. run
b. base
c. strike
d. diamond
e. pitcher
f. glove
g. ball
h. out
baseball

a. trunk
b. tire
c. roof
d. keys
e. engine
f. jack
g. hood
h. fan
car

**page 86**
a. pupils
b. pens
c. class
d. rulers
e. examination, exam
f. subjects
g. English
h. papers
school

a. wing
b. fly
c. ticket
d. trip
e. seat
f. air
g. pilot
h. land
airplane

**page 87**
222: Burns, math
223: Lee, computer
224: Miller, history
225: Johns, art
226: Smith, Latin

Sally: Jane, Dick
Joe: Maria, Sam
Mary: Paula, Pete
Tom: Theresa, Chuck
Sarah: Bev, Gus

**page 88**
Store 1: Mac, grocery store
Store 2: Phil, drugstore
Store 3: Leroy, barbershop
Store 4: Alice, card shop
Store 5: Henrí, pet store

dog: Jane, ranch
horse: Dave, farm
cat: Carmen, apartment
fish: Tomas, town house

**page 89**
Rick: cab, NYC
Pete: train, Philadelphia
Sam: plane, Chicago
José: bus, Las Vegas
Ralph: trolley, San Francisco

Lane 1: B.J., Camaro, third
Lane 2: Drag, Trans Am, second
Lane 3: Race, Mustang, fourth
Lane 4: Willlie, Toyota, first

**page 90**
General: 15, U.S., WWII
Major: 5, France, WWII
Captain: 4, North Korea, Korean
Sergeant: 3, England, WWI
Corporal: 1, Laos, Vietnam

Banker: lilies, April
Lawyer: daffodils, September
Doctor: roses, October
Singer: carnations, June

**page 91**
Stan: 4, Presbyterian, Africa
Larry: 7, Methodist, Ireland
Clyde: 3, Lutheran, Switzerland
Charles: 12, Mormon, Denmark
Art: 9, Catholic, Belgium

Channel 2: "Guess My Job," Barney
Channel 5: "Rummy," Bob
Channel 7: "Clues," Burt
Channel 9: "Win a Trip," Billy
Channel 11: "Deal 'Em," Buzz

**page 92**
Diane: Skippy, terrier
Nancy: Fido, mixed
Marla: Fifi, poodle
Kathy: Cinnamon, chow chow
Ann: Rex, German shepherd

Mary: senior, floor exercises, Penn State
Megan: sophomore, balance beam, Ohio State
Maxine: freshman, uneven parallel bars, University of Virginia
Molly: junior, vaulting, University of Maryland

**page 93**
1. climate (151)
2. division (6)
3. mixer (9)
4. summer (2000)
5. accelerate (200)
6. taxing (11)
7. midline (551)
8. accident (201)
9. driver (4)
10. icing (101)
11. advise (506)
12. omission (1001)

**page 94**
Saturday, February 4th

**page 95**
Monday, January 21st

**page 96**

| N | I | G | H | T | E | L | D | I |
|---|---|---|---|---|---|---|---|---|
| A | K | M | R | A | D | U | L | T |
| Z | W | R | O | N | G | G | A | A |
| E | N | E | A | R | N | O | B | L |
| D | E | T | L | I | E | O | U | L |
| I | S | T | Y | A | V | D | Y | R |
| E | R | O | A | E | P | E | A | C |
| O | L | C | S | E | R | A | L | H |
| P | C | S | U | M | M | E | R | T |

**page 97**
1. bottle—$1.05, jar—$.05
2. 19 = XIX. Take away the I and you have XX (20).
3. 18 days; he jumps all the way out on the last day
4. 3
5. 7
6. he, her, here, ere, rein, in, I

**page 98**
1. the Pacific Ocean; It was the largest ocean even before it was discovered.
2. 1; After eating one cracker, your stomach isn't empty.
3. It wasn't raining.
4. holes
5. because he earns double giving two haircuts vs. one
6. by serving mashed potatoes
7. halfway because after she is halfway in, she is coming out
8. meat
9. It was still light out when she went to bed.

**page 99**
1. the letter U
2. the letter i
3. invent
4. lounger
5. 9
6. the letter E
7. the letter G
8. 10 cents
9. 9
10. the letter i

**page 100**
1. The doctor is his sister.
2. Pete is Chuck's son.
3. your mother
4. the son's mother
5. No, because it's his mother.
6. No, if she is a widow, he is dead.
7. Danielle's uncle
8. his father
9. her nephew, his brother

**page 101**
1. set
2. sea
3. store
4. tea
5. teas
6. ten
7. tease
8. teaser
9. ore
10. ores
11. rot
12. rots
13. rote
14. roe
15. nest
16. net
17. nets
18. east
19. ease
20. sane

**page 102**
1. queen
2. turtle
3. windy
4. acorn
5. restaurant
6. picture
7. flippers
8. valley
9. bicycle
10. rotten
11. different
quintillion

**page 103**
1. lion, den
2. Idaho, Boise
3. flame, paper
4. oak, acorn
5. happiness, smile
6. baseball, glove
7. circus, clown
8. hearts, jack
9. June, Monday
10. cold, snowy
11. Pacific, Nile
12. Franklin, electricity
13. house, den
14. cat, kitten

**page 104**
1. flounder, worm
2. steak, coffee
3. dinner, cake
4. granite, copper
5. college, English
6. couch, satin
7. carton, cereal
8. hockey, puck
9. August, Tuesday
10. hammer, nail
11. salt, shaker
12. jacket, zipper
13. bracelet, emerald
14. bank, money

**page 105**
1. book, magazine
2. purple, green
3. tiger, bear
4. chair, table
5. shirt, pants
6. leg, elbow
7. ten, seven
8. picture, mirror
9. chef, barber
10. maple, spruce
11. baseball, golf
12. robin, wren
13. happiness, anger
14. cake, pie
15. pepper, cinnamon

**page 106**
1. jazz, rock
2. orange, yellow
3. boxing, track
4. slippers, shoes
5. bedroom, kitchen
6. blouse, coat
7. pencil, crayon
8. knife, scissors
9. ship, canoe
10. flounder, tuna
11. shades, blinds
12. sight, smell
13. wasp, ant
14. fork, knife
15. postcard, letter

**page 107**
1. 6, 7, 8
2. 3, 4, 7, 8, 10
3. 8, 10, 12
4. 7, 9, 11, 13
5. 12, 11, 10
6. 14, 12, 10
7. 20, 25
8. 80, 75, 70
9. 40, 50
10. 70, 60
11. 15, 18
12. 21, 18
13. 15
14. 82, 76
15. 16, 20, 24
16. 32, 24, 20
17. 45, 75
18. 24, 32
19. 104, 208
20. 75

**page 108**
1. 62, 59 (x2, -3)
2. 46, 47 (x2, +1)
3. 28, 32 (÷2, +4)
4. 28, 26 (+10, −2)
5. 195, 200 (x3, +5)
6. 14, 22 (-4, +8)
7. 90, 110 (÷2, +20)
8. 98, 92 (÷3, -6)
9. 43, 86 (+5, x2)
10. 44, 42 (-3, -2)
11. 64, 32 (x4, ÷2)
12. 43, 129 (-5, x3)
13. 122, 118 (÷2, -4)
14. 60, 64 (+12, +4)
15. 81, 162 (+3, x2)
16. 595, 594 (x5, -1)
17. 9, 14 (-2, +5)
18. 168, 504 (+6, x3)
19. 160, 480 (-5, x3)
20. 86, 172 (+10, x2)

**page 109**
A. evidence
B. throne
C. maid
D. eon
E. takes
F. moats
G. shag
H. tooth
I. ties
J. is
K. dime
A mistake is evidence that someone has tried to do something.

**page 110**
A. night
B. minute
C. floor
D. house
E. that
F. woman
G. fork
H. hurt
I. oat
J. ha
A minute of thought is worth more than an hour of talk.

**pages 111-112**
Answers will vary.

**page 114**
1. blue, unhappy
2. money
3. omelet
4. bicycle
5. rodent
6. square, rectangle
7. caution, slow down
8. closed-in spaces, small spaces
9. Romeo
10. cub
11. sidewalk
12. shirt
13. *The Wizard of Oz*
14. west
15. digest food
16. swallow
17. library
18. sauerkraut
19. ocean
20. furniture, floor

**pages 115-119**
Answers will vary. Some possible answers are listed here.

**page 115**
1. finger, hand
2. White House, Washington, D.C.
3. red, tomato
4. cave, bat
5. graphite, pencil
6. black, licorice
7. flashlight, battery
8. radio, listen
9. Boise, Idaho
10. banker, bank
11. curtain, window
12. cold, ice cream
13. beans, vegetable
14. toes, foot
15. boat, water
16. ten, eight
17. tree, maple
18. dress, woman
19. helmet, football
20. walk, man

**page 116**
1. turtle, reptile
2. letters, words
3. sand, desert
4. leaves, green
5. strings, guitar
6. ball, bat
7. dry, powder
8. Big Ben, England
9. Navy, water
10. Reader's Digest, magazine
11. mouse, rodent
12. food, eat
13. feet, people
14. dog, canine
15. oar, rowboat
16. aftershave, man
17. adult, grownup
18. cold, ice
19. wheels, car
20. milk, dairy

**page 117**
1. dogs, bones
2. light, day
3. hand, glove
4. goldfish, bowl
5. shaving cream, face
6. siren, police car
7. golf ball, hit
8. bed, sleep
9. grass, lawn
10. wolf, howl
11. Paris, France
12. frown, unhappy
13. cold, winter
14. elbow, arm
15. cuff, pants
16. editor, book
17. bed, bedroom
18. bowl, soup
19. bracelet, wrist
20. petal, flower

**page 118**
1. Paul Newman, Bill Clinton
2. eye, ear
3. toes, fingers
4. pretzel, water
5. picture, sound
6. bench, nail
7. body, teeth
8. up, left
9. tire, wing
10. paper, metal
11. February, November
12. tissue, lightbulb
13. snow, blood
14. hamburger, ham
15. robin, trout
16. President, Pope
17. writer, actor
18. lemon, sugar
19. time, date
20. breakfast, dinner

**page 119**
1. dog, chair
2. word, number
3. 7, A
4. London, Paris
5. sing, read
6. coal, snow
7. button, zipper
8. truck, feather
9. spaghetti, chow mein
10. pedal, tire
11. morning, noon
12. Colorado, California
13. happy, sad
14. 1000, 100
15. animal, weather
16. west, north
17. bee, robin
18. pool, trail
19. happy, sad
20. cap, helmet

**page 121**
1. bad conditions, gunmen inside
2. dark and by the way the building looks
3. She couldn't see anything electrical working inside.
4. night
5. She saw them go in.
6. safety, smarter to wait for backup

1. at the supermarket
2. late afternoon, early evening
3. lots of people shopping for dinner
4. drove, had to look for a parking space in the parking lot
5. what to have for dinner
6. yes, *Children* implies more than one child.

**page 122**
1. hot, sunny
2. noon, The sun was directly overhead.
3. 3-4 hours
4. no, They were hungry and they didn't have any food.
5. They were tired of hiking.
6. east

1. noon
2. Wednesday
3. summer, woman needed her air conditioning repaired
4. eating lunch
5. so he could move her car to work on it
6. get alternate transportation, complain to the manager

**page 123**
1. provides an unwanted dog with a home
2. two: mother and child
3. to see how the puppies reacted to the child
4. size, temperament, appearance, gender of dog
5. less chance of having problems (e.g., biting)
6. apartment or house; chose a smaller dog

1. dinner for guests
2. anniversary, birthday, holiday, promotion
3. yes; because they "hope everything will be perfect"
4. yes; "people began coming in" implies lots of people
5. no
6. evening

**page 125**
toothpaste
baseball
shark
chicken

**page 126**
screw
eye
coat
worm

**page 127**
cat
flashlight
person
wrist

**page 128**
mouse
bird
goalpost
doghouse

**page 129**
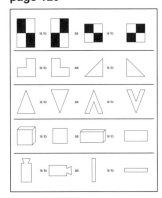

**page 130**
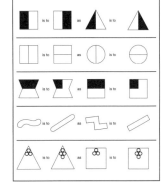

**page 131**
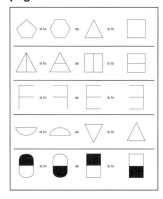

**page 132**
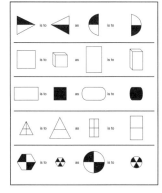

**page 133**
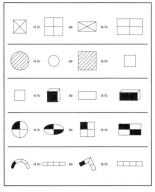

**page 134**
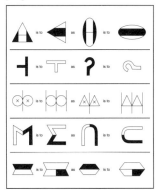

**page 135**

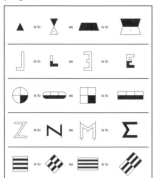

**page 139**

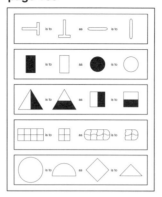

**page 144**
17
13

**page 145**
15
13

**page 146**

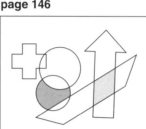

**page 151**

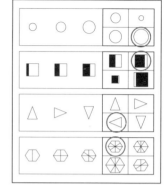

**page 136**

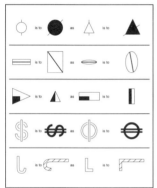

**page 140**

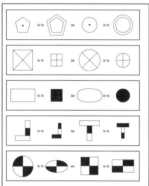

**page 147**

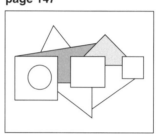

**page 152**

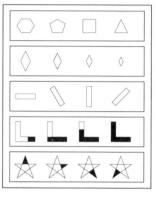

**page 137**

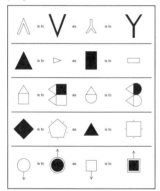

**page 141**

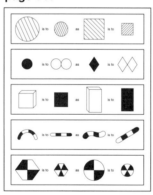

**page 148**

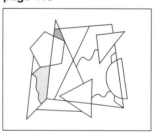

**page 153**

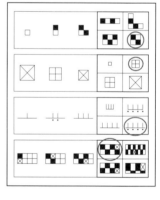

**page 138**

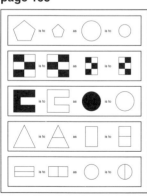

**page 143**

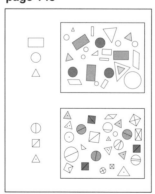

**page 149**

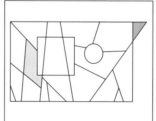

**page 154**

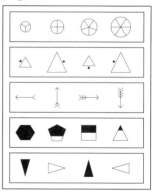

**page 155**
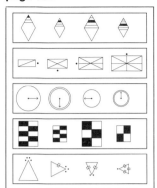

**page 156**
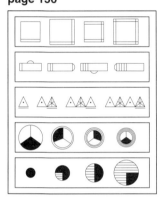

**page 157**
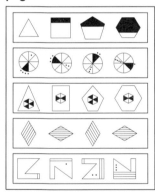

**page 158**
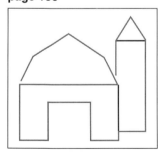

**page 159**

**page 160**
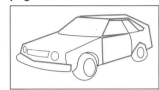

**page 161**

**page 163**
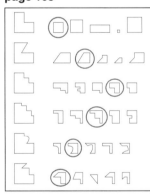

**page 164**
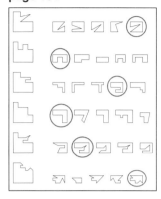

**page 165**
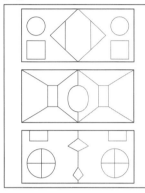

**page 166**
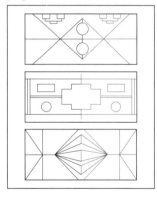

**page 167**
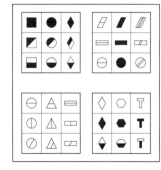

**page 168**
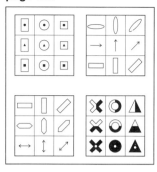

**page 169**
horseshoe/mug on shelf
different picture in frame
flame on candle
box/bowl
book label in different place
longer cabinet on wall
fringe on rug
fewer trees outside
drawer pull different above
 the bed
extra wrinkle on bedspread
throw pillow stripes going a
 different way
clock shows two different
 times
clock on wall/picture on wall
one panel on closet door
 is different
closet handles are different

**page 170**
trees by corral are different
gate is open
two horses in corral
tractor
more bushes by house
more windows on house
black window on top story
smoke from house blowing
 a different way
two cars on the road
top of silo a different color
apples not on one tree
golfer's pants change color
golf flag
two golf balls

**page 171**
lawn mower and rake in the yard
mailbox at end of driveway
bush/plant by garage door
windows on garage door
shape of window on side of garage
smoke from chimney
chimney made of brick/stone
curtains at windows
window different on front door
more windows
different windows on front of house
birds vs. clouds in sky

**page 172**
leaves are different colors
bird has different colors
rabbit has more whiskers
two rabbits
deer drinking
two large rocks by rabbits
size/shape of lake
more clouds
different sun
more trees
plants in water
snow on mountains

**page 173**
plant: over-watered or not watered enough
dog: sick dog, getting shots
couple: getting married
deli: had a fire/vandalism

**page 174**
police: speeding
table: morning, breakfast foods on the table
tire: ran over a nail/glass
man: wrong food/food not cooked right; He will get a new meal.

**page 175**
report card: all As and one F, surprised to get an F
couple: lost; They are looking at a map.
boy: sick; taking his temperature, medicine nearby, holding a tissue
dog: He is hungry.

**page 176**
bed: looking for something
cat: The boy is about to step on the cat's tail; the cat will meow and run; the boy will feel bad.
pot: The pot is boiling over; the heat is too high.
bus: She wants to get on the bus.

**page 177**
drugstore: stocks medical needs, not musical needs; No Admittance sign
map: Mexico and Canada are reversed, USA is misnamed
boy: different sleeve lengths, different pant lengths and different material on pants, missing a shoe
watch: 5 hands, two buckles, wrong numbers

**page 178**
headstone: RSVP instead of RIP, no February 31st, date of death written wrong, died 10 years before he was born
clinic: backward numbers on door, says "No Cats or Dogs Allowed" but it's a vet's office, no handle on door
car: steering wheel on hood, tree on roof, square tire, front door is upside down
washer: buttons mislabeled, picture of eyeglasses on panel, two doors, dishes inside instead of clothes

**page 179**
chair: half rocking chair, half cushion, head rest not done
letter: address/stamp/return address in wrong place, zip code incomplete, says "Don't Handle with Care," phone number instead of zip code
stove: mislabeled knobs, different burners, knobs on door, front looks like a clothes dryer
road: sign says "No Cars Allowed," sign says "Merge Right" but road merges to the left

**page 181**

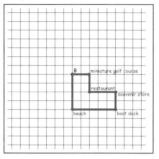

1. 2 miles
2. west
3. 18 miles

**page 182**

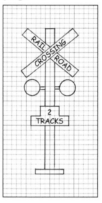

**page 184**